£6.50

D1095410

Alpine Club Guide Books

BERNESE ALPS EAST

ALPINE CLUB GUIDE BOOKS

Bernese Alps East

MÖNCH – EIGER – FIESCHER
FINSTERAAR – SCHRECK – LAUTERAAR
WETTERHÖRNER – OBERAAR – GRIMSEL

compiled and edited by
ROBIN G. COLLOMB

Alpine Club London

BERNESE ALPS EAST

First published in Britain 1979 by
The Alpine Club   London

Copyright © Alpine Club   1979

SBN   900523 27 1

Designed, produced and sold for the Alpine Club by
West Col Productions   Goring   Reading   Berks. RG8 9AA

Produced from computer information storage and retrieval systems
developed from the first edition and its residual unpublished
material issued under the title Selected Climbs in the Bernese
Alps (Collomb) 1968

Serial 81A, September, 1978

Revised and re-written in two volumes as -
Bernese Alps Central (1979)
Bernese Alps East (1979)

Printed offset in England by Swindon Press Ltd, Swindon, Wilts.

Contents

Abbreviations   8

Note on diagrams   9

Introduction   11

    Extract from prefatory note to 1968 edition - note
    to 1979 edition - Maps - Altitudes and nomenclature -
    Orientation - Winter and ski ascents - Camping -
    Grading of climbs - Mountaineering terms, language
    and glossary

Valley Bases   19

    Grindelwald valley   19
    Reichenbach valley (Rosenlaui)   21
    Haslital (Meiringen to Grimsel Hospice)   21

Huts and other mountain bases   23

MÖNCH and EIGER   36

FIESCHER-WANNEN-FINSTERAAR group   68

SCHRECKHORN-LAUTERAARHORN chain   110

WETTERHÖRNER   133

ROSENLAUI-GAULI-BÄCHLI basins   146

UNTERAAR-OBERAAR-GALMI basins   153

Addenda   165

Index to routes shown on diagrams   168

General Index   171

Diagrams

Jungfraujoch S side   35
Mönch SSE face and NE face   38
Mönch NW face   43
Trugberg E side   46
Mönch and Eiger from W   49
Eiger SE face   54
Eiger Nordwand (NW face)   56
Eiger N face   59
Fiescherhörner from WNW   69
Fiescherhörner from SE   72
Fiescherwand   74
Fiescherhörner (Ochs) E-NE side   82
Ochs Fiescherhorn NW face   87
Grünhorn group from SW   92
Gross Wannenhorn from NNE   94
Finsteraarhorn W side   100
Finsteraarhorn-Studerhorn from ESE   102
Finsteraarhorn-Studerhorn from NE   104
Schreck group from SW   111
Schreckhorn S face   115
Schreck group from N   120
Lauteraarhorn S face   132
Wetterhorn SW side   135
Wetterhörner from S   139
Wetterhörner from NE   145
Oberaar glacier basin looking W   156
Scheuchzerhorn-Escherhorn from NE   159
Galmihörner from SW   163

ABBREVIATIONS

AACB	Bern University Alpine Club
approx.	approximately
biv.	bivouac
c.	circa (approximately)
E	East
gl.	glacier(s)
Gr.	Gross(e)
h.	hour(s)
KF	Kümmerly & Frey (map)
Kl.	Klein(e)
km.	kilometre(s)
L	left (direction)
LK	Swiss federal map
m.	metre(s)
min.	minute(s)
mtn.	mountain(s)
N	North
O.	Ober
pt.	map spot height, point (literally) on a route
R	right (direction)
Rpt.	report from correspondent, personal communication
rte(s).	route(s)
S	South
SAC	Swiss Alpine Club
sta.	station
U.	Unter
W	West

Other compass directions are indicated as: NE, NW, SE, SW, etc.

NOTE ON DIAGRAMS

Several diagrams in this guide have been drawn in outline only, in those locations where additional route information may be included in later editions with a minimum alteration to artwork, e. g. Grimsel glacier basin. Other diagrams have been treated halfway between the latter scheme and absolute completion because they overlap information pertaining to the companion volume 'Bernese Alps Central', e. g. Jungfraujoch S side.

Not all routes, and sometimes mountains, are represented in diagrams. Cost economy and popularity have been taken into account. Nonetheless, diagram coverage in relation to routes described is considered fairly comprehensive and it is hoped that a few omissions will not inconvenience climbers using the guide.

The Addenda at the back of this volume includes notes on the differences in spot heights, spelling, etc. observed on the new 1/25,000 map, sheet 1268 entitled Lötschental which was only published in May, 1978, and affects some of the information published in the Bernese Alps Central volume.

Spelling on diagrams agree in general with the new 1/25,000 map. This applies particularly to new phonetic spellings for many place names. Much as some of these offend traditional spellings, they have been largely used on diagrams while old and new spellings are given in text descriptions. However a few are so offensive (with which Swiss mountaineering authorities concur) that we have retained the old in diagrams and text, merely noting in text the current map spelling. In a few cases it is thought that spellings on the map are simply wrong, and in these cases we have retained the traditional names which still appear on the 1/50,000 map.

Introduction

EXTRACT FROM PREFATORY NOTE TO 1968 EDITION

The Bernese Oberland is a name used generally to describe the mtn. range flanking the N side of the Rhone valley from Martigny to Brig and Grimsel. Strictly speaking the mtns. of the Bernese Oberland are the true highlands of the Canton of Bern. As such the name applies only to the N side of the range. The S side, facing the Rhone, belongs to the Canton of Valais, and the watershed of most of the highest peaks marks the boundary of the two political divisions. The range is therefore more correctly described as the Bernese Alps.

The range is orientated roughly W to E. In this direction the mtns. rise progressively in altitude, extend in glaciation and become generally more complex and interesting at the eastern end. The chief mtn. groups in the western and lower half are the Diablerets (3210m.), Wildhorn (3248m.), Wildstrubel (3244m.) and Altels-Balmhorn (3699m.), which are described in the Bernese Alps West guidebook. This section ends at the Lötschenpass (2690m.), midway along the range. Beyond this point lies the finer central and eastern sections which are the subject of this guidebook.

In modern times the reputation of the Bernese Alps has been mainly confined to the notorious North Wall of the Eiger. The publicity given to this mtn. has undoubtedly worked against the broader and truer mountaineering values of the region. The Bernese Alps are still regarded by many climbers as a series of long glacier 'trogs', or a place where fashionable skiing is practised in winter. In fact this great range offers an unusual variety of snow/ice and mixed climbing, from the simple to the very serious, and in this sense it is the finest region in the Alps for acquiring a classical experience of mountaineering. It also has more big ice climbs than any other region in the Alps.

The most striking features of the range are the size of its glaciers - the largest in the Alps - and the number of picturesque snow peaks. The latter tend to be found 'inside' the range, while the steepest walls and rockfaces, and mixed rock/ice peaks, are found on or near the perimeter. The famous walls of the Jungfrau, Eiger and Wetterhorn, likened by Leslie Stephen to a huge wave breaking over the valleys of Grindelwald and Lauterbrunnen, are composed mainly of limestone. The 'inside' peaks, such as the Schreckhorn and Bietschhorn, are usually composed of gneiss, and the rock is often good.

In so large a region it is inevitable that no single centre will provide a satisfactory base for making expeditions in all parts of the range. Grindelwald comes nearest to meeting this requirement; Kandersteg is better placed for climbing at the western extremity of the central zone, and Belalp and the Lötschental are in the best position for approaching the big mtns. situated more to the SW and S. At the eastern end of the range the Grimselpass approach will prove useful for a number of peaks or particular routes in the Finsteraarhorn neighbourhood.

The NE corner of the range, between Rosenlaui and Meiringen, is noted for the small and compact limestone chain of the Engelhörner, an exclusive rock climbing area, which is the subject of a separate guidebook.

The weather in the Bernese Alps is traditionally regarded as the worst of all the 4000-metre zones of the Alps. There are good meteorological reasons, reinforced by the N-facing escarpment of the range, for assuming that this will always be the case. On the other hand prevailing bad weather affecting the Bernese Alps is almost certain to affect the Pennine Alps, for example, to a similar degree.

PREFATORY NOTE TO 1979 EDITION

We are now able to publish a much expanded, as well as revised, guide to the Bernese Alps which necessitates two volumes - Central and East - having a logical division at the Jungfraujoch. While most of the material has been stored and updated for 10 years, the main task has been the production of 60 new illustrations to accompany the texts.

A number of peculiarities pertaining to the Bernese Alps need to be emphasised. The very extensive glaciation of the range has undergone still further shrinkage, making the problems sometimes acute with crevasses, potential avalanche conditions, stonefall activity and generally icy conditions or icy rocks where good snow was formerly found. We have gone to some length in texts to emphasise these problems where they are known to exist, but caution should be exercised everywhere. Readiness to adapt to conditions different to those indicated in the guide, and having the initiative to appreciate these matters quickly, are requirements for making safe and successful ascents in the region. Always endeavour to obtain local information about current conditions before setting out on a climb.

The high standard of ice climbing now demonstrated in the range reflects the tremendous advance made in ice climbing techniques during the last decade. The wide variety of ice climbs is perhaps the most attractive feature of the range to the modern mountaineer. The runaway number of ascents in the 1970s may leave the impression that former standards were overrated, but this is not the case. If anything these climbs are technically harder now than when, for example, Welzenbach's parties were pioneering some of them in the 1930s. It follows that objective dangers are more serious as well.

13

The overall grading of routes has only been modified at the top end of the scale, and this is mostly due to accommodating rising standards in the six categories of difficulty available. The discussion about introducing a seventh grade in the Alps continues but nothing is settled. Numerical rock grading standards remain much as before.

The complete grid of the new Swiss LK map in 1/25,000 has now been published. So many sheets are involved that sheet numbers are given for most entries in the guidebook. It need hardly be added that this map is a superlative production, despite a few curious spellings and some detail at variance with the 1/50,000 map.

In common with introductory remarks in the new Pennine Alps guide (1975-79) and Mont Blanc Range (1976-79), mountaineering is now such an expensive pastime that no purpose is served by giving an indication of costs, or advice in detail on how to travel to the various centres in the Bernese Alps. Road and rail communications in Switzerland are among the best in Europe. The nearest international airports are Zürich and Geneva. Motorways in Switzerland are generally free of toll charges. Swiss rail/air holiday tickets have half a dozen vouchers entitling the holder to substantial reductions on mtn. railways and cableway journeys.

Similar comments about huts apply. Reciprocal rights on charges continue to exist between various Alpine countries but there have been problems with this scheme in Switzerland and there is resentment about the soaring hut occupancy figures for non Swiss Alpine Club members, others with foreign club cards of which they are not nationals, and tourists in general. Everyone is asked to be on their best behaviour when staying at Swiss huts and to cooperate with wardens on eating and sleeping arrangements. Alpine Club reciprocal rights now recognised over most of the Alps do not as yet (1978) extend to Switzerland.

MAPS

The guide is designed for use with the new Swiss federal grid map (LK) drawn in a scale of 1/25,000. Equally good is the LK 1/50,000 map which comes in a grid series and tourist series, but naturally it has features only half the size and reduced detail. A super-tourist version of the latter and a tourist map in a smaller scale covering the entire range are issued by Kümmerly & Frey (KF), the main LK agents in Switzerland. Maps of 1/100,000 are of little value for climbing but may be useful for planning. The following maps cover the entire Central and East areas (all available from West Col Productions).

LK 25m. in horizontal bands W-E, arranged N-S (10 sheets):

	1228 Lauterbrunnen	1229 Grindelwald	1230 Guttannen
1247 Adelboden	1248 Mürren	1249 Finsteraarhorn	1250 Ulrichen
	1268 Lötschental	1269 Aletschgletscher	1270 Binntal

LK 50m. in horizontal bands W-E, arranged N-S (6 sheets):

	254 Interlaken	255 Sustenpass
263 Wildstrubel	264 Jungfrau	265 Nufenenpass
	274 Visp	

LK 50m. Tourist sheet 5004, Berner Oberland. Does not include Bietschhorn, Nesthorn, Belalp or lower part of Aletsch group, and restricted Grimsel approaches. Another edition of this map is issued by KF under ref. no. 0634. It has a red overprint to emphasise walking routes, hut approaches, etc.

LK 100m. 37 Brünigpass 42 Oberwallis

KF 75m. No. 0630. Berner Oberland, Lötschberg, Oberwallis. This is the best map in one sheet covering the entire Bernese

Alps and all approaches into the range.

A research series of maps in a scale of 1/10,000 of the Aletsch gl. basin was published in 5 sheets by LK between 1962-64. The coverage extends from the Mönch, Jungfrau and Fiescherhorn in the N, down to the Lötschentaler Breithorn, Nesthorn and Eggishorn in the S. These maps contain many additional spot heights, notably of steps/pitches on ridges, and of points along edges of hanging gl., etc. The maps are drawn in a less graphic manner than the new 1/25,000 map. One or two access pts. have been extracted for descriptions in the guide, otherwise additional data on these maps has been ignored.

ALTITUDES AND NOMENCLATURE

All heights are taken from LK 25, either from fixed points or contour calculations extracted from this map. Place names come from the same map, but traditional forms are used where the map shows a phonetic spelling; however the latter is always quoted in descriptions.

ORIENTATION

The directions left (L) and right (R) in the sense of direction of movement of the climber - ascent, descent, traverse of slope - have been used consistently throughout. For mtn. features such as glaciers, couloirs, rivers, etc. the traditional orographical reference to left and right banks as viewed in the direction of flow, i.e. downward, has been abandoned, due to the number of complaints received over the confusion this system causes. These features are therefore now described in the sense of movement of the climber. For example, you go up the L <u>side</u> of a glacier, which was previously described as ascending the R bank. In some descriptions both ways are given to emphasise orientation. Compass directions are also given to assist route finding.

WINTER AND SKI ASCENTS

Generally first winter and ski ascents are mentioned only for the most important summits, judged mainly on height of the mtn., and winter ascents of important snow/ice climbs or modern technical rock climbs. Noteworthy solo ascents are also included as are British ascents at any time of the year. The inclusion of this information is not altogether uniform and we apologise in advance for any omissions.

CAMPING

All the valley bases (see next section) have authorised camp-sites, and the impecunious seeking cheaper camping can usually find 'authorised' sites with limited facilities for nominal charges.

GRADING OF CLIMBS

In accordance with the UIAA classification system, the grading of rock climbs is numerical from I to VI and A1 to A4 for artificial. Grade I is the easiest and VI the hardest. Variations of difficulty are denoted by + and - signs; plus is above the normal rating and minus below (i.e. V-/V/V+). These variations above grade IV will matter for the expert climber and should be equally helpful in the lower grades for the average performer. It must be stressed that the grade of a climb is determined not only by pure technical difficulty but also by objective danger and length.

Mixed climbs and snow/ice climbs are also graded in six stages. This grading is always more approximate and less precise than the numerical rock grades because of variable conditions in a season and from year to year. Winter climbing will be different again, and apart from severe cold grades could be lower or higher according to the nature of the route. In order of rising difficulty: F (easy), PD (moderately difficult), AD (fairly difficult), D (difficult), TD (very difficult), ED (extremely difficult). Further refinement is possible by adding plus or minus signs.

MOUNTAINEERING TERMS, LANGUAGE AND GLOSSARY

For the most part terms used in this guide, though not always proper English words, will be known and understood by alpinists. A glossary is considered unnecessary. The Swiss unit of currency is the Franc, divisible into 100 centimes. Good currency exchange facilities exist in all valley resorts, at banks, hotels, stations and tourist offices. Warning: the old axiom that the Swiss will take any currency for goods and services rendered no longer applies - it ceased in the late 1950s. You must tender in Swiss francs.

Valley bases

GRINDELWALD VALLEY

This is the foremost centre for mountaineering in the Bernese Alps. The train journey from Interlaken takes 30 min., following the branch line up the Black Lütschine valley. The village is very large and spread out W-E over a distance of 2 km. Several large carparks. The station (1034m.) is at the W end (junction with branch line going up to the Kl. Scheidegg). There is a bus service to the Wetterhorn hotel at the E end of the made-up road in the direction of the Gr. Scheidegg, to which there is also a service road. Several dormitories for climbers, one with camping in adjoining field. Other campsites over one km. from centre. Those who want to pay more have over 100 hotels and pensions to choose from. Inquire at tourist office.

The First chairlift (2167m.) starts from Gydisdorf near E end of village and gives access to many excellent training walks on the Schwarzhorn ridge which encloses the valley to the N; classical views of the great Oberland peaks. The Pfingstegg cableway (1392m.) gives a modest start to the long trek up to the Strahlegg hut. The mtn. railway via Alpiglen to Kl. Scheidegg runs frequently, and on foot the walk takes 2 h. This railway is the most expensive in Europe. The link from Kl. Scheidegg to the Jungfraujoch, through a tunnel inside the Eiger, is 9 km. long. Trains operate up and down at least 12 times a day. The train journey from Grindelwald to Kl. Scheidegg takes 35 min.; from Kl. Scheidegg to the Jungfraujoch (q.v. huts section), 50 min.

UPPER RHONE VALLEY (GOMS)

From Brig the valley is served by the main line rack railway and a postbus service; frequent trains and buses. In a few km. the village of Mörel (759m.) has a cableway to the Riederalp (hotel, 15 min.). At the next halt, Betten, another cablelift goes up to Bettmeralp (1933m.) on the long traverse path (jeep road status) between Riederalp and the Jungfrau hotel above Fiesch. Fiesch (1047m.) is a pleasant holiday resort with all the usual services at the entrance to the Fiesch valley. Cableway in two stages to a forepeak (2893m.) of the Eggishorn (2926.7m.), one of the classic tourist viewpoints for the Aletsch gl. From the halfway station (2212m.), in 15 min. along the traverse path, the famous Jungfrau hotel (2182m.) is reached. This path continues to Märjelensee (2300m.), the main entrance hereabouts to the Aletsch gl., to which a road from Fiesch has been proposed recently (1977), but there is considerable opposition to the scheme. The Finsteraarhorn hut is reached from Fiesch by a long but well marked route.

Continuing up the valley, the road and railway come to a string of small villages; Niederwald (1251m.), Blitzingen (1293m.), Selkingen (1317m.), Biel (1312m.), Ritzingen (1318m.), Gluringen (1336m.), Reckingen (1326m.), then Münster (1371m.), the largest village in the valley above Fiesch. After the hamlet of Geschinen (1351m.) one reaches Ulrichen (1346m.) which has an excellent campsite, $\frac{1}{2}$ km. down the Nufenenpass road, alongside the Rhone itself. Now in the top of the valley are Obergesteln (1355m.) and Oberwald (1368m.), from where the road zigzags to the L and the train engages rack and pinion to reach Gletsch (1757m.). Road junction for Grimsel and Furka passes. No main services at Gletsch apart from hotel accommodation. The railway continues to the Furka. The branch road winds up to the W in several long zigzags to the Grimselpass (2165m.), hotel, etc. From here motor vehicles can be taken along the contractors' road to the dam wall of the Oberaarsee (Berghaus Oberaar). The Grimsel Hospice lies below the summit of the pass on the

REICHENBACH VALLEY (ROSENLAUI)

From Meiringen (595m.) on the main road and railway (terminus, Innertkirchen) in the Haslital, this valley opens immediately to the S, leading up to the Gr. Scheidegg which communicates with the Grindelwald valley. A narrow metalled road (postbus) starts at Willigen hamlet (621m.), across the main river bridge outside Meiringen, and twists up steeply into the valley bed to reach Rosenlaui hamlet (1328m.). Hotel, food shop, a few guest houses, limited services. The road continues to a bridge just below Schwarzwaldalp (1462.3m.). Beyond that is a farm/jeep lane towards the Gr. Scheidegg (1962m.), not for motorists. The private Broch hut (1499m.), marked on map, is reached by a slip road NE from pt. 1441m. just below the bridge at Schwarzwaldalp.

The main feature of the middle Reichenbach valley is the limestone cliffs and spires of the Engelhörner (the subject of a separate guidebook) while the upper part is dominated by similar walls forming the Wellhörner and Scheidegg Wetterhorn.

HASLITAL (MEIRINGEN TO GRIMSEL HOSPICE)

Meiringen (595m.) is a small town where the enclosed upper part of the Haslital commences. The railway continues only to Innertkirchen (625m.), but there is a regular bus service up the good valley road, via Innertkirchen, Guttannen (1057m.) and Handegg (1401m.) to the Grimsel Hospice (1980.2m.) below the Grimselpass. There is an interesting series of smooth glaciated rocks in the upper part of the valley, which is a huge water catchment area for hydro-electric schemes. All the lakes in and on either side of the valley have been raised by dam walls. Innertkirchen is the starting pt. for the Gauli hut (Urbachtal), Handegg for the Grueben hut, and the Stockstägen contractors' cableway sta. (1703m.), near the road, for the Bächlital hut. A funicular railway at Handegg goes up towards the Grueben hut. The Grimsel Hospice is a somewhat bleak place to use as a base centre. Bunkhouse accommodation available. Taxi hire, e.g. for Berghaus Oberaar. Motorboat service to W end of Grimselsee.

Huts and other mountain bases

Kleine Scheidegg   2061m.

1   LK 1229.   Virtually a resort for sightseers on the Grindel-wald-Lauterbrunnen railway.   Batteries of telescopes for those inclined towards Eiger-watching.   A large hotel and various smaller establishments with bunkhouse accommodation, shops, etc. The Jungfraujoch railway starts here.

Eigergletscher Station   2320m.

2   LK 1229.   First halt on the mtn. railway from Kl. Scheidegg to the Jungfraujoch, at entrance to the tunnel inside in the Eiger. Hotel with bunkhouse accommodation; generally handy for the Eiger normal rte.

Jungfraujoch Station   3454m.

3   LK 1249.   The station, hotel compartments, etc. are built inside the mtn. and windows are flush with side of ridge facing S down the Jungfraufirn.   The hotel section has been rebuilt since a bad fire in recent times.   Arrangements in the hotel for cheaper dormitory accommodation change from time to time.   In 1975 the expensive bed & breakfast rate had been abolished.   There are half pension rates inclusive dinner. Certain club organisations in 1977 were having heated discussions over rising costs for climbers who are otherwise prepared to accept rough quarters. The situation will change again.   Dormitory accommodation is still provided (several rooms) for sleeping purposes only; the rooms are normally locked between 09.00 and 17.00. One of the dormitories may be converted temporarily and according to demand to a self-service restaurant. Self-catering in dormitories is forbidden but climbers may make meals in the cold tunnels linking various parts of the underground system.   There is one long tunnel leading E to the outside on the Jungfraufirn, and another with a staircase going W to a gallery giving access to the Jungfrau-joch itself.

Guggi hut   2791m.

LK 1229, 1249.   SAC.   Situated on a rocky spur forming the lower part of the Mönch NW ridge. Normally no warden, door unlocked, fully equipped 30 places. Water supply is a problem and it is often necessary to descend about 5 min. to the nearest snowpatch. The direct approach from the Eiger gletscher sta. is rarely the best way to the hut because the gl. is usually in poor condition.

4 From Kl. Scheidegg follow the large path S on a broad grass spur towards the Eiger Gl. sta. Shortly before this bends sharp L (E) up to the sta., turn off R along a lower path working still lower by another branch (2203m.) round a corner SE to reach the Eiger gl. N bank moraine ridge c. 100m. below a large prominent rock on its crest (45 min.). This point is 10 min. in descent from Eiger Gl. sta. The rte. is now well marked with red paint flashes. Go S diagonally down moraine and smooth slabs to the Eiger gl. stream (2162m.), cross it then scramble up scree slopes and broken rocks SSE to pass c. 200m. L (E) of the old hut (2388m.). A R-hand fork, painted sign, goes to old hut (annexe for new, poor facilities). The main path continues up L side of the ridge, finally slanting R (SW) to reach hut on the spur crest (3-3½ h.).

Mittellegi Hut 3355m.

LK 1229. Owned by the Grindelwald guides, rough quarters in a unique position atop a knoll on the NE ridge of the Eiger, and reserved exclusively for that ridge. No warden, door unlocked, fully equipped but take a small stove, 16 places. The approach from Grindelwald via Bäregg and the Kalli (Challi) is only used by those who must avoid the Jungfraujoch railway fare (6½ h.).

5 From the Eismeer sta. (3159.7m.), the last halt before the Jungfraujoch terminus, go through a window on to a ledge (metal spikes) and descend a cut path with ladder/ropes in the rockface for 40m. to the gl. below. Beware of stonefall. Traverse normally without difficulty N and NE along the sloping Challifirn gl. terrace, a few large parallel crevasses, stonefall from impressive SE face above you, for nearly 1½ km. to the broad snowfan cutting into the side of the ridge below the hut. The last third of this traverse can be very icy in late season. Go straight up the snowfan, sometimes crevassed, and the rocks above its apex where the holds and ledges shelve outwards (II-), then by easier mixed snow and slabby rock trending R to the ridge and hut (2 h.). PD.

Alternatively, when the Challifirn is icy. On passing the second small snow bay inlet (the 1st being under the SE face proper and the 2nd under the Mittellegi Gr. Turm on the ridge high above), climb on to the rib marking the R side of the 2nd inlet and almost immediately ascend diagonally R in a long rising traverse across the side of the ridge, over ledges and terraces, broken at one third distance by a couloir above the 3rd inlet. After this pt. rise somewhat more steeply to cross a flat rib high above the broad snowfan, and finish by traversing almost horizontally not far below the ridge crest to reach the hut (2½ h.).

Bergli Hut 3299m.

LK 1249. Bärglihutte. SAC. The hut is perched on a rock rib near the top of the Fiescher gl., not far below the U. Mönchjoch. Normally no warden, door open, fully equipped, places for 20. The long classic approach from Grindelwald via Bäregg and the Kalli (Challi) is almost completely disused today (8½ h.).

6 From the Jungfraujoch sta. take the long E tunnel to the Sphinx exit (3460m.) on to the upper part of the Jungfraufirn. Cross the snowfield NE to the O. Mönchjoch saddle (3629m.), normally large track in mid season (1 h.). On the other side descend slightly and cross the head of the Ewigschneefeld to reach in the same direction the U. Mönchjoch (3529m.), finishing up a steep snow slope (30 min.). On the other side descend sometimes badly crevassed slopes due N to reach the top of a rock rib. Go down this with a little track to hut (30 min. , 2 h. from Jungfraujoch). F+.

Note: The approach from the Eismeer sta. (3159.7m.) across the upper Fiescher gl. (called by LK, Obers Ischmeer) is dangerously crevassed. While no distance at all, 2 h. or more might be taken to penetrate the labyrinth, working due S then round in a circle to the L (E) to reach the hut from above. Not recommended.

Konkordia Hut   2850m.

LK 1249. SAC. A collection of buildings on a rock corner pedestal at the centre of the largest gl. system in the Alps. The terrace below the Fülbärg (Faulberg) overlooks the Konkordiaplatz gl. junction. The present main hut is the result of several enlargements and rebuilding. Hotel service, warden and staff, 100 places. Second hut, 30 places.

7 From the Jungfraujoch sta. take the long E tunnel to the Jungfraufirn exit. Initially cross the snowfield E then descend S and SE, keeping somewhat L of centre. Covered crevasses can be troublesome as far down as 3000m. and parties should be roped. The lower part has bare ice patches and is normally wet and unpleasant. Follow moraine across entrance to the Grüneggfirn and reach rocks below the hut. A marked path with rails ascends the rock corner to hut (3 h.).

8 The approach from Belalp up the Aletsch gl. is easy but long and laborious. Not recommended (5½ h.). Parties coming from the upper Rhone valley will find the most pleasant rte. by using the Eggishorn cableway from Fiesch to its halfway sta. (2212m.). From here by the large traverse path N, tea houses and rest places, round the Tälligrat shoulder (2386m.) to Märjelensee (2300m.) where the Aletsch gl. is joined. Then a longish walk up its ice and moraines to the hut promontory (about 4 h.). A road is projected from Fiesch to the Märjelensee, to which there is considerable opposition at present (1978).

Finsteraarhorn Hut   3048m.

LK 1249. SAC. The most enlarged hut site in the Bernese Alps since World War II (places for 25 in 1947). Situated romantically on a small buttress at the SW foot of the Finsteraarhorn, beside the Fiescher gl. and facing the Grünhornlücke. Warden and restaurant service, provisioned by aircraft, 115 places. Like the Mutthorn hut site, spring skiers are inclined to arrive by aircraft - a luxury that most summer visitors could not afford.

9 From Konkordia hut (3 h. from Jungfraujoch, Rte. 7) descend the rocky path to the Konkordiaplatz. Turn NE along the Grüneggfirn keeping to the centre, and reach the broad saddle of the Grünhornlücke (3286m.) ($1\frac{3}{4}$ h.). On the other side go straight down snow slopes with a few crevasses and cross the Fiescher gl. to the rocks on which the hut stands conspicuously. From a snow bay on the L follow a track R in the rocks to hut. Normally large trail all the way in mid season ($1\frac{1}{4}$ h., 3 h. from Konkordia, 6 h. from Jungfraujoch). F.

10 From Fiesch, the traditional approach, long but not unpleasant. Local bus or taxi from Fiesch to Fieschertal hamlet (1108m.), saves 30 min. This road may be continued for several km. in the future. Continue down a lane NW to the Brigge(n) chalets and stay on the R side of the river for another 10 min. to a bridge on the L. Cross this and follow the L side with black and yellow waymarks to a tributary stream in a few min. The path goes up the L side of this (signpost, Märjelensee) above a little wooded gorge, and follows the stream direction N, keeping R at a junction, to cross the Seebach (1598m.) and reach a little rockband, at the top of which the path zigzags up to Stockalp (1917m.). Below these chalets the path forks. Take the lower branch to N, away from Stockalp, and marked by red and white flashes. Continue up a narrow horizontal hollow between rockbands, and at the N end descend to the Fiescher gl. near pt. 1908m. (2 h.).

Follow L side of the stone covered gl. towards the inlet of Flesch (2028.6m.), rough biv. shelter for excellent local rock climbs. Pass below this then move R to avoid a badly broken zone in the gl. Return immediately L and mount the first rocks, waymarked, of the Bergi, to a grassy terrace running above the gl. Follow this with a track and descend to pt. 2130m. where a moraine band leads to another steeper broken section of ice above inlet 2248m. (2½ h.). Go up the L side between the ice and rocks, with traverses on rock well marked by paint flashes. Continue close to the L side, sometimes on the rocks, to pt. 2572m. (1 h.). A little higher, go straight across the next flat section NNW with large crevasses and so reach moraine under the Finsteraarrothorn on the other (now N) side of the gl., about pt. 2880m. on LK 50 map. Alternatively, work further R (due N) across the gl. to the foot of the S spur, called Rotloch, of the aforesaid peak, and continue up moraine strips on this side. Work along this side of the gl. to rocks below the hut. Just beyond them enter an inlet and go up a snow slope to exit R by a cut path to the hut (2 h., 7½ h. from Fieschertal hamlet).

Stieregg Inn   1650m.

LK 1229. Privately owned, situated about 2¼ h. from Grindelwald along Rte. 11. Bed and breakfast service.

Strahlegg Hut   2687m.

LK 1229, 1249. SAC. A chalet style building situated on the true R bank of the upper icefield of the Grindelwald gl., at the SW foot of the Lauteraarhorn. A very important mountaineering base. The building was destroyed by an avalanche in 1977. A new hut, almost certainly larger and of more modern design, is due to be completed in 1979. Former details: warden with simple restaurant service, places for 50.

11 From Grindelwald sta. go through the village and take the first road turning R after passing the First chairlift sta. In a couple of min. reach the Pfingstegg chairlift (see below). Bear R and at the bottom cross a bridge to follow a steep path L (road to R, ignore) to Halten, beyond which the path is less steep. Reach a junction, fork L and go up zigzags in forest, then R to join the Pfingstegg path (1386m.), and along this under the Mettenberg cliffs to the Bäregg inn (1652m.) (1¾ h.). Signposts for Bäregg all the way.

Continue by the pleasant path round a corner to the Stieregg inn (1650m.), then round the prominent corner of Bänisegg (1807.3m.) (1 h.) to traverse E not far above the gl. by moraine to the Rots Gufer, where rails are fixed to the cliffs. Normally the limit for Grindelwald walking parties. Climb steep rocks above the icefall and at the top continue near the gl. until a move L leads to another barrier thence the Schwarzegg ruins (2¼ h.). Cross the entrance to the Schreckfirn along a moraine with cairns and skirt round a barrier at the far side to the R, to reach moraine again. A clearly marked little path with snow patches now leads above the gl. to the hut (1¼ h., 6¼ h. from Grindelwald).

By using the Pfingstegg chairlift to 1392m. you save 45 min.

Gleckstein Hut   2317m.

LK 1229. SAC. A large and comfortable hut on the SW slopes of the Wetterhorn, high above the Upper Grindelwald gl. Warden, hotel service, places for 100.

12 From Grindelwald sta. go to the Wetterhorn hotel (1223m.), road with local bus service, private cars permitted, 50 min. on foot. From here take the Gr. Scheidegg lane, being the upper or L-hand of two almost parallel lanes at the outset, and follow it for a few min. round a double bend to a path and signpost on R (NE). Follow the path over pasture towards the foot of the Wetterhorn cliffs. Make a sharp turn R below the cliffs, well marked, and work SW over a series of terraced limestone cliffs with old handrails to the corner at Engi (1670m.). The path continues high above the gl. with occasional handrails, until a further steep ascent of rocky bluffs leads to the upper pastures at pt. 2151m. The path goes NE then NW still fairly steeply to the hut (3 h. from Wetterhorn hotel).

A slightly shorter way by Halsegg (1348m.) and the gl. itself depends on the condition of the ice and is less frequently used; however normally busy with tourists visiting the gl.

Lauteraar Hut 2392.5m.

LK 1230, 1250. Site of the historical Pavilion Dollfus, situated on rocks above the N bank of the Unteraar gl. Warden, simple restaurant service, 50 places.

13 From the Grimsel Hospice (1980m.) descend across the dam wall N and follow a footpath along the N shore of the Grimsel lake to its W end (2 h.). A motor boat service to same point is much more convenient. Continue by the well marked path over moraines covering the ice on the N edge of the gl., and eventually reach an inlet (2099-2140m.) at the E end of the hut promontory. A footpath goes up grass to a pleasant shelf above, which is followed to the hut (2 h., 4 h. all the way on foot).

Aar Bivouac 2731m.

LK 1249, 1250. SAC. Not marked on first edition of LK 25 dated 1974. Marked as 2780m. on 1976 edition of LK 50, sheet 5004 and on grid sheet 264. On LK 1249, situated 300m. horizontally SE of pt. 2751m. (this pt. marked 2764 on LK 5004 and LK 264). This position is a broken rock shelf above the first rockband round the prominent S corner of the Lauteraar Rothörner, marking the junction of the Strahlegg and Finsteraar gls. The biv. hut faces into the Strahlegg section. The hut was destroyed by an avalanche shortly after it was opened in 1974. Rebuilt on a safer and lower adjoining site in 1976. Fully equipped, door open, 17 places.

14 From the Lauteraar hut descend a cut path in rocks to S and reach the gl. below. Cross to the medial moraine and follow it due W towards the junction called Abschwung. Continue, bearing L near the middle of the Finsteraar gl., now going SW along its moraine ribs to the next corner and junction

on R (NW) where the Strahlegg gl. branch enters (2681m.).
Pass R of the latter mound and work R over moraine to the R
side of the Strahlegg branch, approaching pt. 2751m. Turn
sharp R (SE) and follow scree, broken rock and snow horizontally to the hut ($1\frac{1}{2}$ h. from Lauteraar hut). F-.

Husegg Hut   2450m.

15 LK 1250. Privately owned, situated on the NE spur of the
Sidelhorn, close to pt. 2463m., and due W of the Grimselpass
(2165m.). Warden, simple restaurant service, 40 places.
From the Grimselpass (bus) follow the Oberaarsee contractors'
road W for 500m. to a signpost on L, where a path goes up
grassy bluffs to the hut ($1\frac{1}{4}$ h.).

Oberaarsee Inn   2338m.

LK 1250. Berghaus Oberaar. Much frequented spot at end of
contractors' road running from the Grimselpass (2165m.) to
the Oberaarsee dam wall. Restaurant service, places in rooms
and dormitory. Carpark below inn, adjoining dam wall.

16 From Grimselpass (bus) by contractors' road to W, $5\frac{1}{2}$ km.,
$1\frac{3}{4}$ h. on foot. Single track road with passing places open to
private motorists. Taxi service from Grimsel Hospice below
pass.

Oberaarjoch Hut   3258m.

LK 1250. SAC. Situated on the rocks near the bottom of the
S ridge of the Oberaarhorn, just above the narrow opening of
the pass (3223m.). Warden in residence from time to time,
fully equipped, 45 places.

17 From the Oberaarsee Inn (Rte. 16) descend the continuation
road and cross the dam wall to N side of lake. Follow path
along this shore which fades in slabby rocks at the W end (1 h.).
Continue by moraine banks on the Oberaar gl., keeping somewhat R of centre for 2 km., then more or less in the middle
with multiplying groups of crevasses, aiming for the prominent

col at the top. Steepening snow slopes lead to the col. On your R a cut path in rocks goes up briefly to the hut ($2\frac{3}{4}$ h., $3\frac{3}{4}$ h. from Oberaarsee Inn). F, but not for walkers.

Finsteraarhorn - Oberaarjoch huts connection

18 LK 1249, 1250. An important link in the E-W (or vice versa) traverse of the Bernese Alps, frequented by spring skiers and summer touring parties.

From the Finsteraarhorn hut reverse Rte. 10 to the Rotloch corner, below pt. 2843.3m. ($1\frac{1}{4}$ h.). Now go L (NE) into the Galmi gl. branch, keeping L of a badly crevassed central zone till opposite pt. 2928m., where a circling movement R then L is made to avoid another crevassed section. Head N across the Studerfirn, round the toe (3136m.) of the Nollen (not named on LK 25) and go up R (E) over an easy snow slope to the Ober- aarjoch and hut ($2\frac{1}{4}$ h., $3\frac{1}{2}$ h. from Finsteraarhorn hut, 3 h. in reverse direction). F/F+.

19 Parties making this tour often prefer to cross the Gems- lücke (Gemschlicke, 3335m.) because it avoids complications with bad crevasses. Recommended.

Descend from the Finsteraarhorn hut as above, to the broad moraine/snow inlet halfway down to the Rotloch corner. A double stream cuts this large inlet. Ascend a moraine spur on the L (W) side of these outfalls to snow slopes running straight towards the pass at the top, with the Finsteraarrothorn on your R (E). Go up to the gully reaching the pass and climb its bed on snow or ice; alternatively use broken rocks above its R side ($1\frac{3}{4}$ h.). On the other side descend a gentle snow slope with crevasses near the bottom to the Studerfirn where Rte. 18 is joined and followed to the Oberaarjoch hut (1 h., $2\frac{3}{4}$ h., same time in reverse direction). F/F+.

Galmihorn Hut   2113m.

20 LK 1250. Privately owned by the Münster Ski Club, situated WNW of Münster village and reached by a jeep road through the Bann woods. Motorable for small cars. 46 places. Door normally locked. For key, inquire at Münster post office.

Dossen Hut   2663m.

LK 1209, 1210, 1230. Tossenhütte. SAC. The Rosenlaui or northern base for the Wetterhörner group. Situated on the rock ridge between the Gstellihorn and Dossen, overlooking the Rosenlaui gl. Warden, simple restaurant service, 50 places. Being enlarged in 1978.

21 From Rosenlaui hamlet (1328m.) go up the road round the first big bend and after a few min. take a waymarked path on L to the Rosenlaui gl. gorge.   Reach a bridge crossing L (1485m.) over the gorge outlet, and take this to a steep forest path rising E to a junction nearly level with the Gletscherhubel (path to L or N goes to Engelhörner hut). Continue S to old moraine and later ascend zigzags at the R end of a rockband to follow a moraine crest S called the Dossenweg, finishing up a gully with steep walls to a moraine field at pt. 2294m. ($2\frac{3}{4}$ h.). The track veers sharp L round a brim of rocks and gradually bears R again to climb a series of short rockbands SE and a loose couloir with fixed rails, etc., up to the ridge (1 h.).

At the bottom of this section, just above the E edge of the moraine field and under a rock wall a short distance off the track, is found the <u>Rosenlaui biv. hut</u>, opened in 1973, door normally locked, 12 places, fully equipped, gas cooking, etc., for key inquire at Rosenlaui hotel.

Follow the broken rock ridge with a mostly good track to the hut (30 min., $4\frac{1}{4}$ h. from Rosenlaui).

Note: Local guides use a short cut from pt. 2294m., by working SSE up the moraine/snowfield into its top L-hand corner. A steep cut path rises in the rocks above NE, to join the hut ridge not far above the pt. where it is reached by the usual rte.

Gauli Hut   2205m.

22 LK 1210, 1230. SAC. Situated in the lonely, rock-striated Gauli cwm above the Urbachtal.   Normally no warden, fully equipped, door open, places for 34.   From Innertkirchen by small road then a good path, 6 h.   Car drivers can save $1\frac{1}{2}$ h. Being rebuilt in 1978.

Grueben Hut   2512m.

23 LK 1230.   AACB.   An old wooden hut situated above the Arlen cwm (Handegg), on the N side of the Grueben gl.   No warden, door open, fully equipped, 14 places.   Reached from Handegg in the Haslital (bus) by funicular and footpath in $3\frac{1}{2}$ - 4 h.

Bächlital Hut   2328m.

LK 1230.   SAC.   A fine hut serving an interesting secondary area, situated on a large hogsback in the Bächli valley, directly below the Alplistock.   Warden and simple restaurant service, 43 places.

24 From the hydro-transporter cableway sta. called Stockstägen (1703m.) below the Räterichsbodensee dam wall on the Grimselpass road (bus); carparking at a turning off very sharp bend just below dam.

A good path winds up above the dam and enters the valley just below pt. 2157m. Continue past the N side of the Bächlisee, near the stream and cross this L only a few min. from the hut ($2\frac{1}{4}$ h. from road).

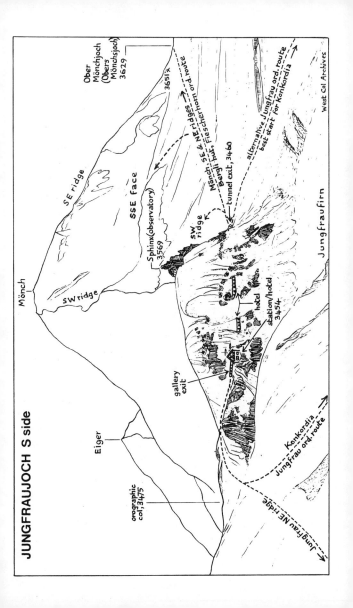

JUNGFRAUJOCH S side

Ober Mönchsjoch (Obers Mönchsjoch) 3629

3651'x

SE ridge

SSE face

Mönch

SW ridge

Sphinx (observatory) 3569

Mönch, SE & NE ridges; Fiescherhorn ord. route

SW ridge

Bergli hut

tunnel exit, 3460

alternative Jungfrau ord. route, best start for Konkordia

West Col Archives

Jungfraufirn

hotel

station/hotel 3454

gallery exit

Eiger

Konkordia Jungfrau ord. route

orographic col, 3475

Jungfrau NE ridge

Mönch and Eiger

JUNGFRAUJOCH   3475m.

LK 1249. In mountaineering, a classic pass, rarely used today because of the mtn. railway. A long sérac barrier extends across the N side but in early season this can be turned without too much difficulty at the W end. The approach is from the Guggi hut by Rte. 138 in the Bernese Alps Central guide. AD. First traverse: H. B. George, J. G. Hardy, R. Liveing, A. W. Moore, H. A. Morgan, L. Stephen with C. Almer, P. Baumann, C. Bohren, U. Kaufmann, P. Michel, P. Rubi, 21 July, 1862.

MÖNCH   4099m.

LK 1249. The middle peak of the "most famous mtn. trinity in the world" (Lunn). This very popular mtn. has some excellent snow/ice climbs, short and long, to suit all tastes. The Bergli hut approaches are treated as variations in favour of the altogether more convenient Jungfraujoch departure point. First ascent: S. Porges with C. Almer, C. and U. Kaufmann, 15 August, 1857. In winter: F. Bischoff, R. Bohren with P. Bohren, P. Egger, P. Michel father & son, 24 January, 1874. On ski: H. Hoek with A. Tännler, G. Moor, 12 November, 1901. West Col Archives Memoir 2722. Rpt. Talbot, 1969. Roberts, 1972, 1976. Anstruther, 1977.

<u>South-East Ridge.</u> The trade route, F+/PD. The upper ridge is thin and exposed but not often corniced. A short, interesting snow climb and the best descent rte. from the mtn. First ascensionists by a variation. As usually climbed today: R. J. S. Macdonald with C. Almer, M. Anderegg, 29 July, 1863.

25 From the Jungfraujoch sta. take the long E tunnel to the Sphinx exit (3460m.) on to the upper part of the Jungfraufirn. Cross the snowfield NE to the O. Mönchjoch saddle (3629m.), normally large track in mid season (1 h.). Ascend a triangular snow slope rising into the broad foot of the ridge, keeping L, and so reach the rock crest below pt. 3887m. Continue on the ridge to a shoulder where the easy-angled sharp snow crest leads nicely to the summit ($1\frac{1}{2}$ h., $2\frac{1}{2}$ h. from Jungfraujoch).

Coming from the Bergli hut, reverse Rte. 6 over the U. Mönchjoch to the head of the Ewigschneefeld. Climb on to the NE spur of the SE ridge just below pt. 3687m. and follow crest of spur to the SE ridge shoulder. Some bad rock under the shoulder, PD, rather pointless.

<u>South-South-East Face.</u> A good snow/ice climb at a nursery distance from the Jungfraujoch. An ice barrier at the bottom is very steep but short. The original line took loose unpleasant rocks in the lower middle part, but it is better and safer to work further L and climb entirely on ice. Start early because surface conditions deteriorate rapidly after sunrise. Climbed frequently in early summer, 400m., main part at 54°, D/D+. Incredibly, the first ascent appears to have been made in 1864 by a Swiss party, as a variation to the SE ridge. British ascent: J.O. Talbot with M. Epp, 1964.

26 Start as for Rte. 25 and leave the main trail after 20 min. to cross snow almost due N, to the foot of the face (50 min.). In the R-hand part ascend the first iceband at its weakest pt., variable, and continue up a fairly steep snow slope towards the first rocks. Cross a normally large bergschrund, trend L on steepening snow or ice to avoid the rocks, then climb direct on a smooth snow/ice slope in the one place where this is possible, between the rocks and the upper séracs further L. An exit schrund is possible. So reach the summit ridge on this side, a few m. from the top ($2\frac{1}{2}$-4 h. from foot of face).

<u>North-East Face.</u> A short but interesting snow/ice climb, similar to Rte. 26 but altogether less serious. Climbed infrequently. About 250m., average angle 52°, AD+/D. First ascent: G.A. Hasler with C. Jossi, 20 June, 1904.

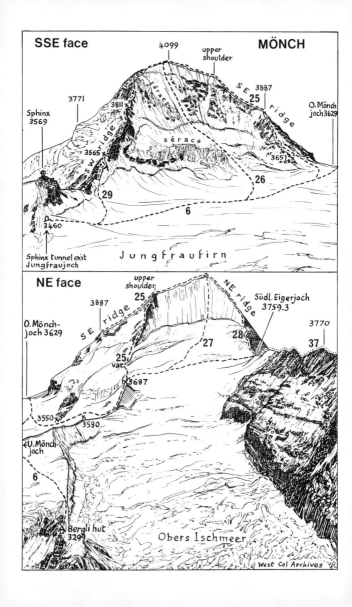

27 From the Jungfraujoch follow Rte. 25 to the O. Mönchjoch then descend slightly to the Ewigschneefeld before climbing up snow to join the NE spur of the SE ridge just below pt. 3687m. Ascend a short distance above the latter pt. then trend R in a rising traverse to a bergschrund at c. 3800m. Cross this and go up more or less directly to the summit in the middle of the face. The schrund can be very difficult and the summit cornice can be large and awkward (4-5½ h. from Jungfraujoch).

North-East Ridge (from Südl. Eigerjoch). A splendid expedition, interesting, mixed climbing, recommended to experienced parties for making a simple traverse of the mtn. PD+. First ascent: G. E. Foster with H. Baumann father & son, F. Teutschmann, 31 July, 1877.

28 Start as for Rte. 27. Instead of ascending towards the NE face bergschrund, traverse NW below the face over crevassed slopes, sometimes awkward, to reach the Südl. Eigerjoch (3759. 3m.) (2 h.). Now climb the mixed snow, ice and rock ridge in a fine position overlooking the NW face. A bergschrund from the L may come right on to the ridge, then two rock steps are climbed quite easily when ice free, to steeper rocks where short difficulties can be turned on L side. The upper ice crest may require a lot of step cutting or good crampon technique (about 2½ h., 4½ h. from Jungfraujoch).

Var: From the Bergli hut follow the var. advised for Rte. 25 and so join the traverse from near pt. 3687m. to the Südl. Eigerjoch.

South-West Ridge. A fine mixed ridge with a few relatively easy technical rock pitches in good conditions. Otherwise the ridge is best climbed in crampons throughout. The most frequented way up the mtn. after the SE ridge. PD/PD+. First ascent: F. T. Wethered with C. Almer and C. Roth, 24 August, 1875.

29 From the Jungfraujoch take the long tunnel to the Sphinx exit and follow the O. Mönchjoch trail for a few min; then move L to join the second little snow saddle in the ridge after the Sphinx, usually defended by a small bergschrund. Ascend below and parallel with crest on its L side, over broken rock and scree, normally snowy, so avoiding small towers on the crest, and pass just below tower pt. 3565m. Continue by steeper slabby rock on L side with two pitches of II, then gradually work on to crest itself. Follow the fine mixed crest, exposed, forming a large buttress whose apex is pt. 3811m. After this cross a small snow saddle and climb the steepening mixed crest again to a rock headwall. Either use a snow/scree ramp slanting L below this to join the NW spur, which is followed in a few min. to top of headwall; or climb the blunt crest direct to same pt., II+ in good conditions. Continue up a fine snow crest to a comfortable slope and trend R up the last bit of snow ridge, sometimes crevassed, to top (3-4 h. from Jungfraujoch).

<u>North-West (Nollen) Spur</u>. A classical Oberland expedition, achieved at an early date and still coveted for its reputation as a great ice climb. In seasons when conditions are good for the rte., sometimes 5 to 8 years apart, climbed frequently. The famous Nollen ice step is usually quite hard, occasionally impossible, and pitches with steps already cut by previous parties makes an appreciable difference to the effort required. Conditions here vary enormously, and pitches up to 60° are possible. AD+/D+. The lower rock section is loose and unpleasant. The climb more or less follows the L side of a snowy buttress in the lower half, and above the Nollen, the R side of the spur. First ascent: E. von Fellenberg with C. Michel, P. Egger, 13 July, 1866. First British (3rd) ascent: A. W. Moore with J. & M. Anderegg, 23 July, 1872. Descended by F. T. Wethered with C. Almer, C. Roth, 24 August,

1875.

30 From the Guggi hut descend 40m. distance to a gap and follow a poor track over scree covered slabs formed in endless short steps shaping a broad hollow. Old fixed wires and cairns in places, tricky in the dark and worth exploring the day before. Work up this zone to the edge of the Mönchplateau (3112m.) (1½ h.). On the L ascend a pleasant snow ridge with outcrops forming two shoulders, up to a broken rock wall extending R and supporting a crevassed snowfield. Climb the rocks close to the ridge line and ascend the steepening snowfield, quite long, trending R to the base of the Nollen (1½ h.). There is a retaining ice wall L, the crest is blunt and concave and ends in a prominent bulge. The R-hand slope is usually steeper. If possible climb the L edge; alternatively make a circular traverse and upward movement from L to R and attack the bulge direct. After two technical ice pitches the angle relents (2-5 h., has been climbed in 45 min.). Continue to a small sloping plateau and from where this steepens trend R up a snow/ice slope along the base of a big ice wall under the summit ridge. Further R cross a bergschrund (stonefall) and go up a pleasant rock rib to the SW ridge (1½ h.) where it becomes a narrow snow crest. Follow this to the summit (45 min., 7-11 h. according to conditions).

<u>North-West (Lauper) Rib.</u> An outstanding mixed climb, one of the best of its class in the Bernese Alps. Much better than any subsequent rte. made on this side of the mtn. It is practically free from stonefall but verglas on the rock sections is common except in perfect conditions and natural protection is poor. The NW face proper is recessed and the rib marks its L-hand edge. An icefall below the rib proper, climbed by the first party, is nowadays avoided by traversing from the NW spur. Climbed over 200 times to date. From the gl. bay under NW face to summit, 950m. Average angle 47°, some

steeper ice pitches and hard rock pitches. TD-/TD. First ascent: H. Lauper, M. Liniger, 23 July, 1921 (15 h. from Eiger gl. sta. direct). Second ascent: A. Bauer with H. Steuri, 20 July, 1934 ($10\frac{1}{2}$ h. from Eiger gl. sta.). Rarely descended (not recommended): 1st. F. & W. von Allmen, 1941. In winter: P. Jenny, R. Stieger, 28-31 January, 1963. Second winter: M. Epp, J. Harlin, 26 January, 1964 in 10 h. First British ascent: J.O. Talbot with M. Epp, 27 July, 1963 (8 h. from Guggi hut, minimal belaying and moving together).

31 From the Guggi hut follow Rte. 30 to pt. 3112m. Go along the ridge edge of the Mönchplateau for a few min. then make a descending traverse L down its supporting snow/ice slope, pitted with friable rocks, about 45° steep, with a schrund at the bottom, to enter the small gl. bay under the NW face ($2\frac{1}{2}$ h.). Cross the bay E and at the R side of a black icy wall climb a steep snow tongue trending R and exit R up a gully on to the hanging snowfield running up from pt. 3218m. An exit L up a steeper gully (nasty) is directly beside pt. 3218m. Ascend the snowfield with increasing steepness, trending L to an iceband closing the top and below a big black limestone wall. A difficult pitch near the L end gives access to the wall. Bergschrund possible below it.

Three snowy shelves slant R across this wall, all petering out halfway up. Ascend trending R towards the more prominent second shelf and follow it, 3m. wide, exposed and awkward with snow/ice problems. The upper end is closed by a projecting rib. In the flank of this rib climb a shallow gully line, verglassed, with the main pitch in an obvious chimney/crack on the R (30m., V), to exit at some flat blocks and a good belay on top of the rib. Above is the overhanging second step of the rampart. Somewhat L, take another chimney/crack giving similar climbing on slightly better rock (25m., V) and reach easier ground near the foot of a steep ice slope section. (A variation is possible to avoid this second hard pitch by

42

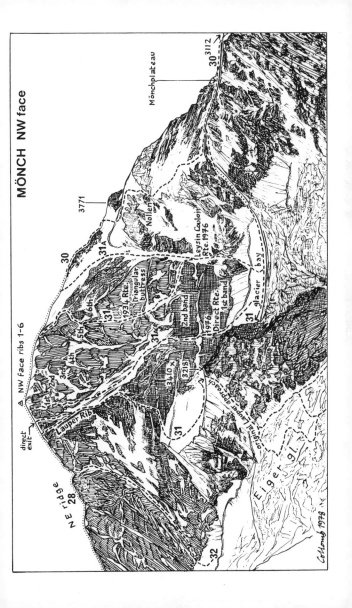

MÖNCH NW face

traversing down R, then reascending L over mixed rock/ice; easier). Climb some awkward boiler plate slabs to a small platform from where the ice slope is embarked upon for several rope lengths, trending slightly L, then up the centre, finally somewhat R to an obvious red gneiss rib. Two pitches on smooth slabs lead to its crest which is followed normally with verglassed climbing to a slight easing in difficulty, where the rib merges gradually into a snow/ice slope. Cross over to the next rib further R and climb this strenuously in three rope lengths to the sharp snow crest of the NE ridge; alternatively keep L on the unprotected ice slope. Finish up the NE crest briefly to summit (8-12 h., $10\frac{1}{2}$-$14\frac{1}{2}$ h. from Guggi hut).

31A <u>North-West Face</u>. A lot of pretentious claims have been made about the merit of "lines" for new rtes. on this face. Relatively narrow, the face is bordered R by a long shallow ice gully, and L by smooth ice slopes and slabs falling from the Lauper rib. The bottom third is closed side to side by a two-tier rockband; above this a narrow mixed snow/ice/rock area; the upper part consists of uneven and more or less parallel rock ribs, five in number, divided by gullies. A sixth rib to the R has a broad triangular buttress supporting it halfway up the face.

The original rte. takes the R-hand bordering gully then crosses the mixed part to join the 5th rib (counting from L). The headwall atop this is turned on R up a gully, so avoiding a direct finish to the summit. A remarkably intrepid expedition for its time, unrepeated. Probably TD, very exposed to stone-fall. Mrs. Hutton-Randolph with P. Inäbnit, A. Rubi, 18 August, 1934. The R side bordering gully was climbed direct (TD) to exit up the big ice slope L of the NW spur exit rib by O. Eistrup, D. Haston, September, 1976. Finally, the lower rockbands were climbed direct using a narrow gully line to join the ice slopes and slabs running up below the upper ribs, these slopes leading towards the exit slope/ribs of the Lauper rte; the latter were avoided by resuming a direct ascent of the steep broken 1st rib which rises in the summit line. ED-. R. Renshaw, D. Wilkinson, 23-26 December, 1976. The directness of this rte. and the German identification some years earlier of its potential value is questioned by several Swiss authorities. Moreover the rtes. are bereft of quality and in most conditions are deathtraps with a higher risk factor than the Eigerwand, for example.

32 North Facet. A barely recognisable rte., starting from the Eiger gl. upper cwm at c. 3350m. and finishing in a couloir reaching little more than halfway up the NE ridge at c. 3900m. TD+ or harder. Derided by the first ascensionists themselves: D. Haston, G. Neithardt, 22-24 December, 1974.

33 West-South-West Facet. An original rte. (1938) takes the W rock facet below the Nollen to join the WSW rib (of pt. 3771m.) which is followed to the NW spur exit rib. Probably D+. A direct ascent of the WSW facet up to below the rock headwall of the SW ridge was made in 1976. TD with pitches of V. Bad stonefall and poor icy rock characterise both rtes.

OBER MÖNCHJOCH   3629m.

LK 1249. Obers Mönchsjoch. A snow saddle between the Mönch and Trugberg, frequently reached or crossed in the course of making climbs in the Mönch-Fiescherhorn area. C. Rohrdorf and party, 27 August, 1828.

TRUGBERG   3932.9m.

LK 1249. A huge rock and gl. spur dividing the Jungfraufirn and Ewigschneefeld. A roughly N-S main ridge carries three elevated summits, of which the main one is triple. Climbed

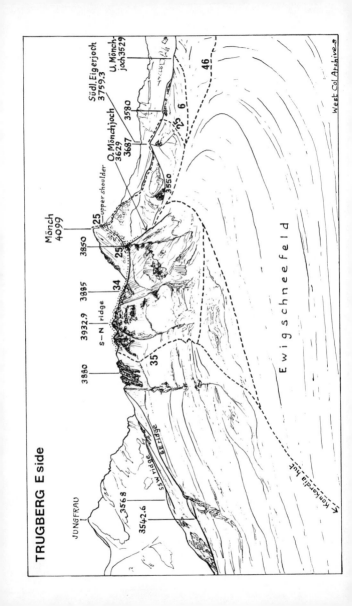

TRUGBERG E side

JUNGFRAU

3568

3542.6

SSW ridge

SE ridge

3880

3932.9 3885

s-N ridge

34

35

Mönch
4099

25
3850

upper shoulder

25

Südl. Eigerjoch
3759.3

O. Mönchjoch
3629 3687

U. Mönch-
joch 3529

3580

25

6

46

3550

Ewigschneefeld

→ Konkordia hut

West Col Archives

not infrequently.   First ascent of highest pt: E. Burckhardt
with P. Egger, P. Schlegel, 13 July, 1871.

<u>Traverse North-South</u>.   A fine narrow ridge with good situ-
ations and plenty of interest, recommended. Excellent regional
views. Some poor rock, mostly quite good. PD+ with numerous pitches of II/II+ and moves of III. First ascent: G. A.
Hasler, Miss M.H. Simpson (Mrs. Hasler) with H. Fuhrer,
7 August, 1906.

34 From the Jungfraujoch reach the O. Mönchjoch as for
Rte. 25 (1 h.). Climb the steepening and narrowing snow/ice
ridge, with a schrund possibly coming across the crest, to an
initial short rock step and take this direct (II+) to another snow
crest leading to a gendarme. Traverse diagonally R on steep
snow/ice and rock, delicate, and return L up a normally icy
slope to crest behind the gendarme.   A little snow saddle
leads to a series of short loose rock steps, fairly easy, then
to the snowcap outpost N summit (3850m.). Continue along a
pleasant level snow ridge to a series of tower/steps. Traverse
these direct, steep pitches followed in turn by easy short descents to little icy gaps, about five in number of which the 3rd
is pt. 3885m. (bits of II). Next reach the start of a more continuous rock ridge, initially mixed, rising to the N top of the
triple summit.   Go up in short pitches directly on the crest
line (II+, sustained) to a craggy shoulder. Similar climbing
with moves of III on the central summit pile leads to the highest
pt.   Some of the pitches can be avoided L ($3\frac{1}{2}$ h., $4\frac{1}{2}$ h. from
Jungfraujoch).

35 <u>Descent</u>. F+ then a long trudge. From the central summit
go down a rock ridge into a gap and up to the S summit tower
top with short bits of II.   Now a short rock crest leads to a
snow shoulder. The true S summit (3880m.) is still some
way along the ridge. Leave the ridge and descend at first

slightly R down a fairly steep snow slope E, soon avoiding a rock projection coming from the L where a bergschrund, normally easy, may appear. Continue down moderating snow slopes due E and parallel with the top of a long slanting ice wall further L, over several crevasses to within sight of a clear run out. To save height now bear L (NE), passing under lower end of ice wall and traverse above a lower rumpled zone on to the Ewigschneefeld. Go up the huge snowfield NW, knee-deep soft snow after midday, to reach the O. Mönchjoch by a reascent at the top of 150m. So return to the Jungfraujoch (3-4 h.).

An alternative descent to Konkordia will be obvious, keeping down the L side of the snowfield to avoid its large terminal crevasse zone.

UNTER MÖNCHJOCH   3529m.

LK 1249. Unders Mönchsjoch. A ridge saddle roughly midway between the Mönch and Walcherhorn (Fieschergrat). See Rte. 6.

SÜDLICHEN EIGERJOCH   3759.3m.

NÖRDLICHEN EIGERJOCH   3614m.

LK 1229, 1249. Two ridge access pts. at either end of the long saddle ridge strung between the Mönch and Eiger. No value as passes. The N col is frequented as an access pt. to the Mönch NE ridge, the S col occasionally by parties going up or down S ridge of the Eiger. See Rte. 37 comment, and Rte. 28.

CHLYNE (KLEIN) EIGER   3472m.

LK 1229, 1249. The head of a large buttress supporting the SW ridge of the Eiger, a pt. reached only by a detour for parties climbing (rarely) the latter ridge. F. W. Oliver, J. O. Outram with H., U. & U. Almer, 7 January, 1896.

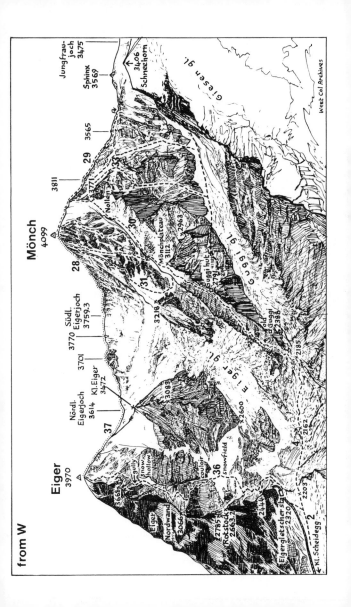

from W

Eiger
3970

Mönch
4099

Jungfrau-
joch
3475

Nördl.
Eigerjoch
3614

Südl.
Eigerjoch
3759.3

37

3770

3701

28

3811

29

3565

Sphinx
3569

3406
Schneehorn

Kl.Eiger
3472

31

30

33

2711

Nollen

gully

snow
hollow

couloir

snowfield

36

x2600

3098

3218

Mönchsplateau
3112

2963

Guggi hut
2791

Giesen gl.

West Col Archives

Eiger
Nordwand
3066

2785

Rotstock
2663

2410

x2600

2185

Gold
Guggi
2388

Guggi gl.

Eiger gl.

Eigergletscher 2320

2203

2162

4

2203

2

Kl. Scheidegg

EIGER   3970m.

LK 1229. With the possible exception of the Matterhorn, more has been written about this mtn. in the department of popular journalism than any other in the Alps, because of its "notorious" Nordwand. It is a fine peak in its own right, essentially severe in character and with few contrasts; it lacks pleasant snow climbing. The rock is mainly limestone, bad to fair, giving varied climbing with intervals on snow or ice. There are no easy rtes. but the ascent has a big tourist following with guides in charge.

First ascent: C. Barrington with C. Almer, P. Bohren, 11 August, 1858. In winter: Messrs. Mead & Woodroffe with C. Jossi, U. Kaufmann, 7 January, 1890. On ski: F. Amacher, W. Amstutz, A. Lunn, W. Richardet, 18 May, 1924.

South-West Flank and West Ridge. The ordinary rte. by which most ascents are made. Formerly well marked with cairns, etc. but the correct way is now difficult to find especially in mist because the cairns are knocked down and few are rebuilt. Similar in this respect to the Hörnli rte. on the Matterhorn and about the same standard. PD. Stonefall danger from parties clattering down carelessly. First ascensionists.

36 From the Eiger gl. sta. follow a track E in moraine then take a ledge L for 100m. followed by short direct zigzags up broken rock below the Rotstock (2663. 2m.) to scree and the lower edge of a snowfield. Climb the snow to an obvious couloir opening at the top L side. Ascend limestone steps just L of couloir to a rockband. Traverse 80m. L and by an ascent and movement R turn the step. Work diagonally L away from couloir to a screefield saddle adjoining the W ridge (pt. 3066m. below). Go up the loose R flank, possibly snowy, and make a steep rising traverse R above the head of the lower couloir; here a traverse L of 50m. along a ledge leads to a spectacular view across Eigerwand. There is a big step in the ridge above. Keep to the rising traverse and go up to an obvious snow hollow on the R side of a buttress flanking step. Near top of snow exit L up a steep gully and shortly move R from it to climb steep broken slabby rock, usually snow/ice covered, in a rising traverse R, still about 100m. below ridge. So reach more continuous snow and climb back towards ridge till opposite a small gap just above an isolated rock step (3668m.). It is usually best to continue up the steep snow/ice slope just below the crest, but for preference reach the ridge itself as soon as possible, cornice on L, and follow it with a loose gully section to top. See also brief descent description appended to Rte. 41 (4-5 h. from Eiger gl. sta. In descent, 2-3 h.).

37 South Ridge. This ridge was described in the previous guide as a practical approach from the Jungfraujoch. However this rte. appears to be rarely followed and we have received no conclusive report from a successful party. The section between the two Eigerjoch saddles is a minor epic and deters most parties. The ridge itself is worthwhile but few parties would contemplate reaching it today up the very badly crevassed Eiger gl. G. E. Foster with H. Baumann, U. Rubi, 31 July, 1876.

South-East (Kalli) Face. A remote precipice easily approached from the Eismeer sta. The rock is generally bad throughout and stonefall frequent except in dry conditions after a period of fine cold nights. The original rte. is less than perfect; it generally follows up near a gully/crack system splitting the face from a pt. below the Eiger NE forepeak down to the upper R-hand corner of the steep gl. inlet at the bottom. A similar crack system comes down in the summit fall line to the upper L-hand corner. The buttress/wall between the two systems has several large roofs across it; these were breached by a tortuous line declared the Direct rte. that keeps R of the summit crack system, to finish between the forepeak and actual top: K. Moser, W. Müller, 24 August, 1974 in 10 h. Pitches of V/V+, A1 (A-1976, 7, p. 64). The original rte. has been climbed about 10 times. 750m., TD-, with pitches of V and one of VI-. First ascent: O. Eidenschink, E. Möller, 11-12 August, 1937. Second: A. Schelbert, G. Steiger, 1964 (7 h.). In winter (5th ascent): K. Haas, W. Müller, E. Ott, M. Wacker, 21-23 December, 1972.

38 Leave the Eismeer sta. as for Rte. 5 and go along the Kallifirn for 15 min. to below the square-shaped inlet under the face. Cross a large awkward bergschrund where it appears most feasible, probably R side, and ascend inlet on steep snow/ice to the top L corner from where the main crack system cuts the face in the summit line. Start at a belt of slabs 25m. R of this pt.

Climb straight up slabs trending slightly R towards the R-hand crack system, as if to reach it at a pt. level with big roofs nearly halfway up the face. After rather more than 250m. of slab climbing (III with bits of IV) reach the L edge of the crack system at the top of its shallow sections, where a large overhanging wall closes it. Traverse R across gully and under wall for two rope lengths, then climb a shallow secondary gully straight above. At 20m. in this a smooth bulging pitch of V. Continue with pitches of III/IV to where the now broader slabby gully gives entry to the huge upper gully in the face, normally very exposed to stonefall. Leave the gully immediately by a short wall and a traverse R of 30m. (V) to reach by a short ascent (IV) a scree terrace. Thus on the front face to R of gully, the next step is climbed direct with a move of VI- (V, with peg) to successively easier pitches on more broken rock to finish some 25m. R of the gully exit on the NE ridge (average 10 h. from foot of face).

North-East (Mittellegi) Ridge. A famous rock climb with an epic history ending with the placing of fixed ropes. The earliest attempt dates from 1874 and later some of the most skilled amateurs and guides of the age were involved in trying to force the ridge - among them Graham, von Kuffner, Hasler, Pfann, Horeschowsky, Amatter, Burgener, Jossi and Emile Rey. "There were not a few who accepted the challenge ... no ridge has so long a record of persistent resistance and remained still unscaled for nearly half a century since it was first tried". (Matsukata). The rte. has always been fashionable, especially with ladies, and it now has the air of a tourist's outing. All the same the gendarmes are very steep, exposed, and mostly of poor rock; the climbing is always serious and competence on rock is essential. The fixed ropes, last renewed in 1974, are strenuous - with these the standard is AD in good conditions.

Descended by M. von Kuffner with J. M. Biener, A. Burgener, A. Kalbermatten, 31 July, 1885. First ascent: Yuko Maki with F. Amatter, S. Brawand, F. Steuri, 10 September, 1921. Amatter led throughout and the guides were paid 1000 francs each. Maki contributed most of the cost towards erecting the first hut on the ridge three years later. Second ascent: Frln. K. Amatter, B. Tännler with A. & P. Inäbnit, F. Kaufmann, 19 September, 1926 (a few days after fixed ropes had been placed by descending from the top). First British: Miss D. J. Lloyd with F. Amatter, F. Sater (also descended by ridge), 18 August, 1928. In winter: F. Amatter, F. Kaufmann-Almer, 12 February, 1934.

39 From the Mittellegi hut an easy almost level snow/rock crest leads in a few min. to the first gendarme/step. Climb this by the crest on poor rock and continue on the crest or just L of it over two more steps, narrow and exposed (II+) into a small gap. Fixed ropes hang on all steep sections. Go up to the foot of the Grosser Turm (3692m.) or 4th step and take it direct with a bulbous overhanging finish, very exposed, fixed rope on crest to its level top. Now go down into a relatively deep gap by icy rock on crest or R of it, abseil from stanchion convenient. Above is the main ridge step laced with ropes all

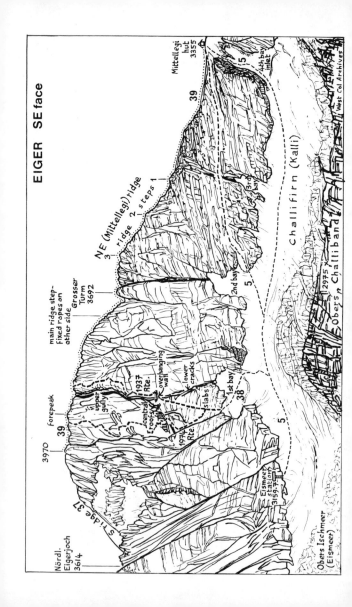

the way up. First a long pitch on the icy R (N) side quite near the crest to a small vague ledge running R. A short distance along this climb direct again by another long pitch to rejoin the crest. All this section is on smooth rock, often ice glazed, similarly the ropes. Continue on the airy crest over numerous short steps, gradually easing off, finally coming to a sharp snow crest. This is quite long, with a forepeak, exposed and normally corniced. It is best to keep R (N) and not try to use rocks below cornice on L (4-5 h. from hut, ascents in 3 h. or less are common enough).

North Face (Lauper Route). A masterpiece of traditional climbing in the free style, mainly on ice but with at least one hard technical rock pitch if the original finish is pursued, and one of the finest rtes. of its class in the Alps. A mountaineering expedition for competent ice climbers. In good conditions, rare enough, a fast party should be able to avoid a bivouac. Conditions have changed since the first ascent and the lower mixed section either needs a lot of good snow or none at all for safety. The upper ice slopes have rarely been found with good snow, forcing several parties off the rte. on to the Mittellegi ridge. Objective danger varies according to conditions but is normally less serious than the Eigerwand. The best starting pt. is Kl. Scheidegg but it is better to sleep out below the face to save time. About 1600m., TD+, although at least one party doing it in ideal conditions put it at TD-.

First ascent: H. Lauper, A. Zürcher with A. Graven, J. Knubel, 20 August, 1932 (13 h. incl. halts). In winter: G. Siedhoff, H. P. Trachsel, 10-12 February, 1964. Solo attempts to date have been frustrated by forced exit to ridge. First British ascent: R. J. Collister, R. I. Ferguson, 17 August, 1976. Climbed about 28 times to end of 1977.

40 Below and to L of face is a broad opening in which hangs the small, irregular Hoheneis (Honysch) icefield. Its R foot

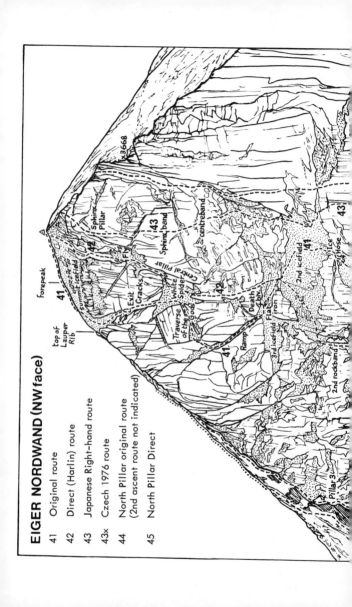

EIGER NORDWAND (NW face)

41 Original route

42 Direct (Harlin) route

43 Japanese Right-hand route

43x Czech 1976 route

44 North Pillar original route
     (2nd ascent route not indicated)

45 North Pillar Direct

is marked by pt. 2204.7m. This is a ledged balcony above an area called Wandflie just below foot of face proper. Further R (SW) is a spot height 2267m., marking end of an isolated rockband under the face. From either Kl. Scheidegg or Alpiglen reach slopes beside an open scree gully with snowpatches between these two pts. and go up to foot of wall. In fact it is more pleasant to traverse in from the R, passing L just below rockband 2267m. Go up to first rockband forming base of wall in a line diagonally L from pt. 2267m. and somewhat R of a line above the gully.

Above a short snowband ascend shaly rock trending R to a series of ledges running L above the rockband. Cross these shelves with low steps L, rising a little, and go round a corner on to the Hoheneis slope. Make a rising traverse L above its narrow ice wall to the other side, not far from its head. Climb loose broken rock steps trending L until you are directly below Mittellegi hut on ridge far above, then ascend fairly direct and gradually R over more snowy steps towards the couloir above the head of the Hoheneis. Reach an overhung ledge line and follow this horizontally R to make a steep rising traverse on snow/ice across the couloir (stonefall), then on rocks to the foot of a large conspicuous rock buttress with a big wall running R and cut at this level by a snowband. Descend slightly R on mixed ground as if to approach the snowband, and reach the L edge of the upper wall. Move up L on loose rock into a big chimney/gully in the L (E) wall, generally icy and exposed but fairly sure on good rock with the exception of a few short overhanging pitches (III+). Waterfall conditions not unusual. An awkward narrowing is turned on L by a smooth delicate slab, wet. The more open upper part may be snow filled and the R wall should be climbed. So reach a steep ice/rock crest at the top. Follow this to the top of its second step, variable either side or on the crest. Good resting place.

Continue slightly L of crest line with another step to more

58

continuous snow/ice slopes above. Commence trending R, passing through a narrow pt. where a tapering rock barrier extends far to the R from the Mittellegi ridge. This rising traverse R over ice slopes is very steep and exposed and leads without gaining much height to a sort of balcony protruding from the face on the dividing line between the N and NW faces. Above, take a short snow/ice crest then an ice slope L of the dividing rib to a narrow strip of rotten rock which is followed up its L side, awkward for two rope lengths, to another ice slope. Trend R up this to a final rock barrier slanting down R and forming on its lower extremity an obvious bulging knob. Climb steep icy rocks to below the knob (IV). This is cut by a near vertical crack, normally ice choked and closed by an overhang. Climb it and force the overhang (V+) to exit on a snow/ice slope. Follow this steeply to more rocks and trend R up these to reach a snow crest forming the top of the rib dividing the N and NW faces. The crest leads pleasantly to the NW ridge at the forepeak with the summit 15 min. away (13-16 h. from foot of face).

Note: About one third of all parties climbing the rte. have managed to avoid the upper rib section when the face was heavily snowed up and stonefall slight by ascending the upper ice slopes directly, well to L of traverse R to balcony. Thereafter turning a broad rock buttress on its L side and returning R on ever steepening snow/ice to go through the upper slanting barrier coming from the NE ridge at a narrow pt. and so reach the final snow crest on R.

Eiger North Wall Original Route (North-West Face). Eiger Nordwand. The history of attempts, accidents and high drama on this face is so well documented in books and articles, albeit an intricate story if brought up to date, that we confine our remarks to practical considerations. For anyone contemplating the ascent it is vitally important to be provided with the best equipment in protective clothing and bivouac/climbing materials. The face has still only been climbed a score of times without a bivouac, and since conditions vary tremendously one bivouac is normally necessary, even for fast and fit climbers, while two is not unusual in bad conditions. If the weather turns then progress or retreat is a grave proposition. The most serious factor on the face is objective danger. Stonefall and sometimes snow/ice avalanches are frequent. There has been an increasing tendency to deride the technical standard of rock climbing; in rarely perfect conditions none of the free climbing exceeds IV+, but most of the time it seems harder, and not keeping to the best rte. in the exit cracks increases the difficulty. Difficulties mount rapidly in adverse conditions. The ideal number is two. One rope of 100m. and two of 50m. are minimum requirements above dispensible equipment.

The Eigerwand is an exceptional climb in every sense and very serious. It has varied problems and superb situations, demanding the application of nearly every technique in mountaineering. ED-. This grading takes account of its great height, 1600m. involving a climbing distance of 2300m., of multiple objective dangers and the seriousness of retreat. "Unofficial" fixed ropes are secured to several bad places but these should be treated cautiously. The rock is friable right up to the 3rd icefield, but better above that. Frequent stonefall occurs at the level of the 2nd icefield, while the 3rd icefield and Flatiron are badly exposed to stonefall. In a storm snow and rocks cascade down all parts of the face.

Climbing history: First ascent: H. Harrer, A. Heckmair, F. Kasparek, L. Vörg, 20-24 July, 1938. Second: L. Lachenal, L. Terray, 14-16 July, 1947. Third: G. Jermann with H. & K. Schlunegger, 4-5 August, 1947. Fourth: L. Forstenlechner, E. Waschak, 26 July, 1950 (in a day, and not repeated in a day for a long time). First winter: W. Almberger, T.

Hiebeler, T. Kinshofer, A. Mannhardt, 6-12 March, 1961. Climbed 23 times to end of 1961.

First British (31st) ascent: C. J. S. Bonington, I. S. Clough, 28-30 August, 1962. Second (38th): R. Baillie, D. Haston, 29-31 August, 1963. First solo: M. Darbellay, 2-3 August, 1963. First descent: P. Etter, U. Gantenbein, S. Henkel, 29-31 December, 1963. By a woman: Daisy Voog and W. Bittner, 1-3 September, 1964. Climbed 52 times to end of 1964.

Climbed in 10 h. by P. Habeler, R. Messner, 14 August, 1974. British winter ascent (4th): D. Renshaw, J. Tasker, March, 1975 (6 days). Climbed over 180 times at end of 1977.

41 At the foot of the face, just R of centre, there is an inverted elongated rock triangle almost surrounded by old snow-beds and avalanche debris. Climb a short gully/depression near the R-hand end (2300m.), cross the snowband above it, trending L, and enter a system of chimneys and cracks rising straight above. This system lies to the R of the First Pillar (2561m.), rising out of the bottom of the face. A chimney then short steps lead in 3 pitches trending R to an obvious triangular snowslope. Follow its L edge to the top then trend slightly L over broken ledges/steps to the foot of the Shattered (2nd) Pillar. Slant easily R to a short vertical rockband (biv. sites) and climb this in 2 short pitches (IV) with a ledge traverse L between them. Continue L by a chimney to the pillar top (avoidable), then straight up an easy snowy rib to the Wet Cave Bivouac below a vertical wall. A fixed rope normally hangs down this. Climb wall, slanting R for 40m. (IV) to reach a small knob on top of a narrow pillar. Above is the Difficult Crack with an undercut base. Take this (IV+, 25m., pegs), then traverse L to continue up a little gully (IV, 20m., pegs), followed by short steps taken in a rising traverse L for 3 rope lengths under large overhanging red walls, to a small triangular snowpatch/ledge. Move up several m. to pegs at the start of the Hinterstoisser Traverse.

Traverse L for 40m. to a niche below an overhang; fixed rope, several pegs. Ignore continuation traverse. Above, climb a chimney/crack (III+, 20m.) and exit L to reach the Swallow's Nest (small, poor biv. site). Traverse L to the 1st Icefield and ascend it direct (45°) for two rope lengths to a big rockband below the 2nd Icefield. On your R is the Ice Hose. Normally the best way is to climb the vertical rockband 15m. L of Ice Hose, to a stance (IV, 12m.); then move diagonally R on to Ice Hose and go up it to 2nd Icefield. Alternatively, from the stance, a traverse L to a little niche, then a diagonal movement L followed by a longer returning movement R brings the top of the Ice Hose to hand (IV and V, sustained, pegs, false peg line at lower level to R). Again, the Ice Hose has been ascended throughout.

Now climb 2nd Icefield direct (45-50°) in 4 rope lengths to its upper edge against rock, and follow this edge for 10 rope lengths to the last rock finger jutting from above into the slope. This is about 50m. distance from the depression separating the Flatiron and nearly 100m. from the latter's crest. There are at least two ways of reaching the Flatiron. Normally best, traverse L on ice for a pitch then breach the wall above by a 5m. vertical pitch, a precise spot in a rockband (IV with peg and sling), to attain a ledgeband with loose stones. Snowy conditions can mask this place. Move horizontally L and go up to the top of a chimney (IV, peg). Continue by a ledge line L, broken at one place (IV, peg), then climb diagonally L on snowy/icy rock to Death Bivouac at the top of the Flatiron and below a cliff. A lower traversing line, normally easier, reaches the crest of the Flatiron one pitch below the biv. and is consequently more exposed to stonefall. Now make a rising traverse L on ice at 55° for one pitch, then almost horizontally across the 3rd Icefield (45-50°) along the ice/rock edge with a short descent at the far end to reach the foot of the Ramp.

Ascend the Ramp for 5 pitches, mixed climbing (IV) to the

foot of an icy chimney (waterfall). Climb it for 10m. (IV+, pegs, strenuous), squeeze 2m. L through a narrowing to an edge, then climb 12m., turning an overhang on the L (IV, pegs, loose). Stance. Continue up an icy gully to the Ice Bulge and climb this direct (10m.) or avoid L by a rock pitch (IV+, pegs, waterwashed), to reach a small hanging snow/ice-field inclined at 45°, overlooking the Ramp below. Ascend it direct for a good rope length, then traverse sharp R to join at a platform the Brittle Ledge at this level, invisible at first. This is the key to the upper face and it must be taken. Go along it for 20m. (II) to a crack and follow this on bad rock, turning an overhang in its upper part on the R (IV, pegs, 18m.). Continue for another pitch to reach the Traverse of the Gods. Good biv. site. Follow this obviously, rising R towards the end (III) and so reach The Spider. Climb an ice bulge (55°) and go up the middle of The Spider on its blunt crest (40°) to its upper R edge. Above to L are two obvious gullies. The R-hand one marks the start of the exit pitches from the face, and it slants diagonally L.

Take a final ice pitch then rocks diagonally L to enter the R-hand gully (IV). Go up over an overhanging block (IV+, peg), then a short dièdre (IV, pegs). Now avoid a blind branch L, and climb two rope lengths in the main snowbed trending R to a white quartz crack below an overhang. Climb this pitch to the overhang and work up L of it to swing L at the top, rope move convenient, then traverse L on steep smooth slabs with another rope move to a terrace with a vertical shallow gully above (from quartz crack, sustained IV, rope moves IV+, pegs, altogether 50m.). It is technically slightly easier to make the slabs traverse L slightly lower down to reach the gully and climb its steep slabby bed for 8m. to the terrace. However this method is unlikely to have the benefit of fixed equipment. From the terrace traverse 6-8m. L to the top of an obvious pulpit. Continue traversing, now going downwards for 10m.

Fixed rope normally in place with short pendulum L at bottom; originally a very awkward abseil. Reach a ledge below a narrow, wet and ice glazed gully. Climb this for 3 pitches, very steep at first then easing a little (IV, III) and reach the top of a low relief buttress. A further 4 pitches up to R of buttress, often ice covered, turning a rock knoll on its R side, leads to near the top of the rock rib dividing the NW and N faces. Either continue direct and R by mainly snowy slopes, or keep L up rock gullies (III). So reach the NE ridge about 200m. distance from summit. Good biv. sites along ridge about 4m. down on S side (20 h. from foot of face in good conditions).

<u>Descent</u>: The upper part is more direct than the cautious way described as Rte. 36. Go down the easy W ridge on snow for 150m. then take a loose gully L with three red abseil pts. in place. At the bottom continue on the ridge, avoiding a step by snow slopes L, then return R under this step and descend trending R on slabs to a conspicuous rockhead, plaque and large cairn. From here traverse 50m. R, then descend a gully L for 150m., lower exit on snow. Now slant R to descend towards the ridge again. Reach a stonefield near ridge; slant down L and descend passing R round rockbands to join a large snow slope L. Descend this to arrive below the Rotstock. Descend trending R for 150m., track appearing, then traverse L along a ledge for 100m. to join snow then a stonefield which leads to the Eiger gl. sta. (2-3 h.).

42 <u>Eigerwand Direct (Harlin Route)</u>. A cooperative internationally sponsored expedition effort using mechanised seige tactics lasting a month, completed by D. Haston, S. Hupfauer, J. Lehne, G. Strobel, R. Votteler, 25 March, 1966; aided by C.J.S. Bonington, K. Golikow, P. Haag, L. Kor, R. Rosenzopf, G. Schnaidt, D.D. Whillans. Climbed despite frequent bad weather and marred by death of John Harlin when a fixed rope broke. Technically a very hard rte., assessed as 11 pitches of IV/IV+, 12 of V/V+, 1 of VI, 2 of A2, 4 of A3. Full description in Eiger Direct, London, 1966. Summary: AJ 71, pp. 256-260.

2nd ascent: Japanese party of 5 commencing 24 December, 1970, ending 21 March, 1971. Some 42 days of this time spent on face using 3000 kg. of equipment and 2000m. of fixed rope, at a cost of over £6000 (at least £20,000 in 1978).

3rd ascent: By 4 Czechs, 3-9 August, 1976. 4th ascent (British/American): A. McIntyre, T. Sorenson, 13-17 October, 1977. 5th ascent, early, 1978.

43 Eigerwand Right-Hand (Japanese Route). Japanese party of 6, using seige tactics, 3 July - 16 August, 1969. Summarised as not as dangerous as Original rte., not as hard as Harlin rte. Repeated in winter by Swiss party after a fortnight's preparation then 6 days on face, January, 1970. Climbed in summer still with seige tactics but only over 3 days by H. Berger, H. Müller, 28-30 July, 1970. A new rte. still further R, and finishing nearly 100m. above pt. 3668m. on W ridge was made by 4 Czechs including a woman, 3-29 August, 1976.

44 Eiger North Pillar. Variously described as N, NE and NW pillar, the latter being more accurate. First climbed by 4 Poles, 28-31 July, 1968 with a very indirect start 500m. to R, then L of crest line to join Lauper N face rte. 2nd ascent, rather more direct: T. Hiebeler, F. Mashke, G. & R. Messner, 30 July - 1 August, 1968. This party turned the lower pillars on L, and climbed closer to crest in middle section. Either rte. in good conditions has no pitches harder than IV+ and crux remains on the Lauper upper rib. Easier and less dangerous than the Eigerwand Original rte. However, bad

rock, and bad for pegging. Poor stances and precarious belaying. Climbed twice since.

45 <u>Eiger North Pillar Direct</u>. I. MacEacheran, A.M. Mc-
Keith, K. Spence, 28-31 July, 1970, after some preparation.
Follows the line of 3 pillars fairly directly, then more directly
in middle section than Rte. 44 but eventually forced off to join
Lauper upper ice slopes. ED, VI, A3/4, bolts. ACG Bull.
1971, p. 31.
2nd ascent, J. Benes, J. Krch, 17-21 February, 1978.

Fiescher – Wannen – Finsteraar group

WALCHERHORN 3692m.

LK 1249. Simple ridge summit on the long NW (Fieschergrat) ridge of the Gr. Fiescherhorn.

GROSS FIESCHERHORN 4048.8m.

LK 1249. A picturesque snow peak with a broad and impressive N face, the Fiescherwand, forming part of the Grindelwald backcloth. The main ridge runs NW-SE and the latter end is marked by the Hinter Fiescherhorn (4025m.). Below the summit cone an elevated snow plateau runs ENE, forming the head of the E part of the Fiescherwand, and culminates in Ochs or the Kleines Fiescherhorn (3900m.), an important satellite top. Its climbs are described separately. The rock is excellent on the ridges and mostly poor on the faces. West Col Archives Memoir 2726, Frischer/Roberts Archives (updated extracts 1978).

First ascent: H. B. George, A. W. Moore with C. Almer, U. Kaufmann, 23 July, 1862. In winter: Mrs. E. P. Jackson, E. Boss with U. Almer, C. Jossi, 11 January, 1888. On ski: J. David, P. König, 22 January, 1902 (two days earlier on snow shoes by G. A. Hasler with C. Jossi).

North-West Ridge (Fieschergrat). The ordinary rte. from the Jungfraujoch, Bergli hut and Konkordia hut, although not so direct for the latter; more direct variations are appended. Long approaches on almost level snowfields, moderately crevassed, with a nice finish. PD. First ascent: H. Woolley with C. Jossi, J. Kaufmann, 31 July, 1887.

46 From the Jungfraujoch cross the O. Mönchjoch by Rte. 6, then cross the Ewigschneefeld to the E, aiming for a broad snow hump adjoining saddle pt. 3613m. on the NW ridge. Ascend easily over slightly crevassed snow slopes to this pt. (3 h.).

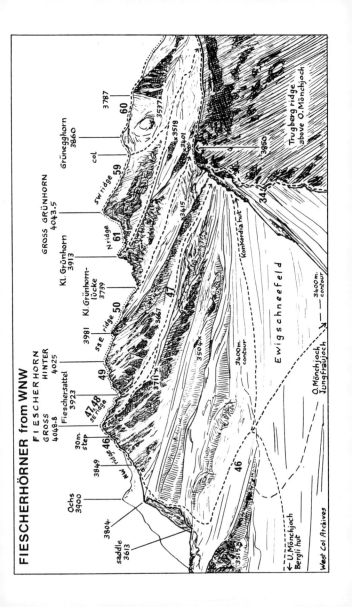

FIESCHERHÖRNER from WNW

FIESCHERHORN
GROSS   HINTER
4048.8   4025

Ochs
3900

3804

saddle
3613

3849

NW ridge

30m. step

46

47·48
SE ridge

Fieschersattel
3923

49

3981

sse ridge

50

Kl. Grünhorn-
lücke
3759

Kl. Grünhorn
3913

GROSS GRÜNHORN
4043.5

N ridge

61

sw ridge

59

col

Grünegghorn
3860

60

3787

3577

3518

3401

3415

3650

341

Trugberg ridge
above O.Mönchjoch

Konkordia hut

Ewigschneefeld

3500

3400m.
contour

3400m.
contour

46

47

3711

3637

3515/3

← U. Mönchjoch
Bergli hut

O. Mönchjoch,
Jungfraujoch

West Col Archives

From the Bergli hut reach the same pt. by Rte. 6 over the U. Mönchjoch ($2\frac{1}{2}$ h.).

From the Konkordia hut ascend the R (E) side of the lower icefall of the Ewigschneefeld, numerous lateral crevasses which may prove troublesome after early August, to the plain middle and upper snowfield. Go up this to 3350m., whence a direct ascent leads to the ridge saddle ($4\frac{1}{2}$ h.).

From the saddle ascend a steep slope to a higher plateau sloping down to the R, and continue keeping R of ridge pt. 3804m. to the foot of the summit ridge proper. This narrows and steepens and is snow with occasional outcrops up to a 30m. step. Climb this fairly direct with short turning movements L, or turn completely L by a steep snow slope positioned nicely above the N face. Finish up rocks on the crest with two short steps and snowy bits to the summit ($2\frac{1}{2}$ h., $5\frac{1}{2}$ h. from Jungfraujoch, 5 h. from Bergli hut, 7 h. from Konkordia hut).

47 From Konkordia it is more direct to join the Fieschersattel and finish up the SE ridge. As for the previous Konkordia approach above, along the Ewigschneefeld to the crevassed slopes running up to the saddle on the L (N) side of rib pt. 3415m. At the top cross a bergschrund and go up a large shallow couloir on rocks and snow to the Fieschersattel (3923m.) (5 h.). Now go up the fine SE ridge on sound rock, climbing or easily turning steps and small towers as desired, to the summit (45 min., $5\frac{3}{4}$ h. from Konkordia hut). The saddle can be avoided and the rock rib on the L side of the crevassed slopes near pt. 3711m. can be joined and followed directly to the summit, PD. First ascensionists ($6\frac{1}{2}$ h.).

South-East Ridge (from Fieschersattel). The shortest rte. from the Finsteraarhorn hut, easy except for the icefall step to the plateau on the NE side of the mtn. PD. First ascent (but not from this side): F. Bischoff with P. Bohren, P. Egger,

10 August, 1871.

48 From the Finsteraarhorn hut descend to the gl. and walk up its R side, crevasses, for 4 km., to below pt. 3443.8m. Beyond, climb the icefall, keeping as far to the R as possible, normally badly crevassed with short snow/ice steps. As the slope eases off work round L (W), still with a few long crevasses, to cross the big gentle plateau strung between the Gr. and Hinter Fiescherhorn. Ascend in the middle to reach the <u>Fiechersattel</u> (3923m.) (4½ h.). In mist the plateau is a bad place for rte. finding. Ascend the ridge as for Rte. 47 (45 min., 5¼ h. from Finsteraarhorn hut).

49 <u>Ridge to Hinter Fiescherhorn.</u> This ridge can be traversed from one peak to the other in 1¼ h. F+. From the saddle (3923m.) turn a tower on the L and follow the pleasant crest to the summit (30 min.). G. Lammer, A. Lorria, 27 July, 1885.

50 <u>South-South-East Ridge of Hinter Fiescherhorn (from Kl. Grünhornlücke).</u> A rarely followed ridge, very fine, narrow, mostly on good rock with little towers and steps, interesting and seldom icy. PD.

<u>Ochs to Gr. Fiescherhorn.</u> This connection is frequented by parties making the round trip including the Hinter of the three Fiescherhörner. PD. W. A. B. Coolidge with C. and R. Almer, 22 July, 1888.

51 From the summit of Ochs descend a sharp snow ridge WSW, normally corniced and delicate, with small outcrops, according to conditions, which leads gradually and in about 30 min. to the large gentle plateau adjoining the head of the Fiescherwand. By keeping L join Rte. 48 to reach the Fiechersattel and SE ridge, thence the summit (1½-1¾ h. from one summit to the other).

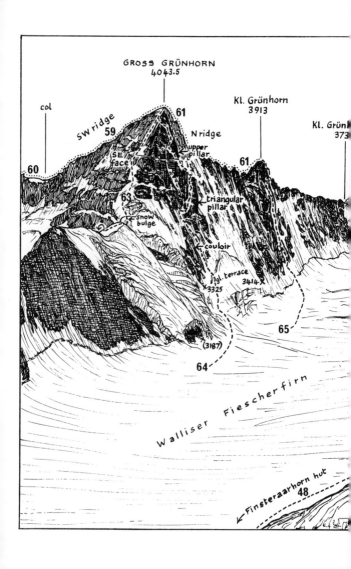

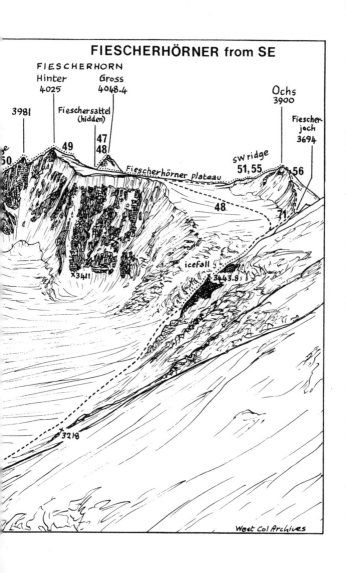

FIESCHERHÖRNER from SE

FIESCHERHORN

Hinter 4025

Gross 4048.4

Ochs 3900

3981

Fiechersattel (hidden)

Fiescher-joch 3694

50

49

47 48

sw ridge 51, 55

56

Fiescherhörner plateau

48

71

×3411

icefall

×3443.8

×3218

West Col Archives

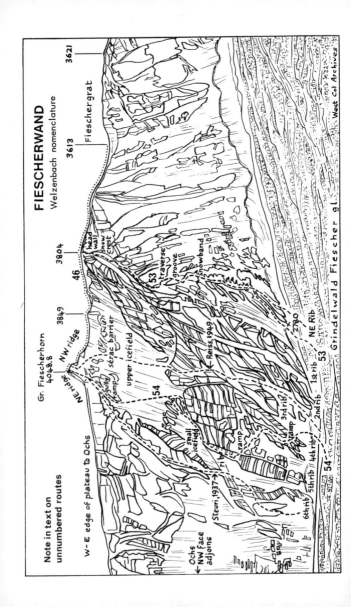

FIESCHERWAND

Welzenbach nomenclature

Note in text on unnumbered routes

W — E edge of plateau to Ochs

Gr. Fiescherhorn 4048.8

NW ridge

3849

3804

46

3613

3621

Fiechergrat

head wall

snow crest

53

traverse

groove

snowband

NE rib

gully

(ramp)

sérac barrier

upper icefield

Reiss, 1949

2790

NE rib

1st rib

53

NE rib

54

3rd rib

2nd rib

ramp

small icefield

4th rib

ramp

Steuri, 1937

5th rib

6th rib

54

Grindelwald Fiescher gl.

Ochs NW face adjoins

West Col Archives

Fiescherwand (North Face).

In English one of the least documented of the great Oberland faces, a fault that may now be rectified. This impressive rock and ice wall is the longest and most extensive belonging to a singular mtn. group in the Bernese Alps; its maximum height equals any part of the more fashionable Lauterbrunnen Wall, and roughly occupies 3 km. x 1250m. The L-hand or E portion belongs rightly to Ochs, regarded in mountaineering as an independent summit.

The R-hand (W) side of the main face is closed by a well defined rib or buttress rising from pt. 2780m. to pt. 3804m. on the NW ridge. A series of parallel upright rock ribs marks the lower half of the face below the summit, and these are closed at the L side by a more continuous blunt rib rising nearly the full height of the face. Between these two confining ribs the upper half of the face consists of a large irregular icefield draped side to side in the top section by sérac bands. These discharge avalanches constantly, but are known to relent in ideal climbing conditions (very rare), and consequently precipitate high stonefall risk as well in the lower parts of the face.

The Fiescherwand is the least frequented of all the Bernese north walls, due to the potential objective danger and to the friable rock which comes out in handfuls. However, there are clear indications that one or more rtes. are now overtaken by events amounting to the dismissal of danger by skilful choice of time and rapid climbing using modern ice techniques.

Guido Lammer wrote in 1886: "The unsolved problem of a direct ascent of the Gross Fiescherhorn by its immense and intimidating wall above the Grindelwald-Fiescher glacier presents the finest, also the most exacting challenge in the Bernese Alps, and only the most resolute mind and most persevering aspirant will succeed in accomplishing this tremendous feat" (from Welzenbach's Climbs, by Eric Roberts).

In 1924 Capt. J. P. Farrar reported that the R-hand rib would be climbable in better conditions than those seen in that year. This tip was picked up by Yuko Maki of Mittellegi ridge fame and by the then unknown F.S. Smythe, but before either could organise an attempt a Dr. Kehl with Fritz Amatter tried in 1926 to climb the face direct and L of the rib. They progressed 250m. before retreating at verglassed slabs. A few days after this attempt the rib itself was climbed by a strong Swiss party (see below). This rte. was repeated by Welzenbach in 1929 following failure the same day on a direct line; he found the rib more difficult than anticipated. Welzenbach was the only real contender for the Fiescherwand direct, which he forced in typically brilliant style the following year.

Long intervals separate subsequent ascents. Three major variations have been made on the lower part of the face, as well as other minor deviations from the original line, while several different exits have been managed. Annual ascents do not occur before 1967. The 1960 British ascent was by the NE Rib.

52 Approach from Grindelwald. Follow Rte. 11 to about half-way between Stieregg and the Bänisegg corner. Make a descending traverse R (S) over grass, then a steep moraine bank, down to the stone covered ice of the Lower Grindelwald gl. Go up this SE with open crevasses, easy, to the little promontory corner (1806m.) of the Zäsenberg. Ascend loose moraine just R of this pt. and join a track running L (E). Follow this above a stream running in a little rocky defile to a corner where an old shepherd's hut is found (1948m.). The classic Zäsenberg biv. site. However it is better to continue to a more respectable height. The track now climbs SW and soon returns L to fade in the upper stream bed. Follow this roughly with grass patches through a series of shallow gullies, bearing R (SW) into a moraine and rock hollow with snow patches beside pt. 2382m. Excellent biv. sites either here or lower down on grass with running water. Several old stone shelter walls built by previous parties (5 h. from Grindelwald).

From this biv. site. (A) Move SW on to an obvious terrace of the Fiescher gl. and follow this WSW for one km., then ascend S to the large gl. bay under the Fiescherwand. This entry is complicated by fairly steep crevassed slopes, sometimes involving wide detours (2 h.). (B) In good conditions the gl. is more easily dealt with as follows. From near pt. 2382m. ascend through snow/rock/scree bands and terraces E for 15 min., then return R to a sloping gl. terrace at a higher level, under pt. 2635m. Follow this terrace SW, keeping fairly high, and pass just below pt. 2652m. to reach along a narrow crevassed snow strip the broader entrance to the gl. bay under the Fiescherwand ($1\frac{3}{4}$ h.).

Fiescherwand (North-East) Rib. The huge buttress marking the R (W) side of the face and defined between pts. 2780 and

3804. Relatively sheltered from stonefall and not threatened directly by séracs this rte., the first made on the face, gives a mountaineering expedition in the classic mould on rock, ice and snow. The crest line in the top half is dislocated L of the line in the lower section. Sustained difficulties on all kind of terrain. The rock is often snow covered or verglassed and varies from poor to fairly good. Several technical pitches on steep ice and with a normally troublesome snow/ice ridge near the top. TD-/TD with pitches of IV+, 1000m., average angle 53°. First ascent: W.H. Amstutz, P. von Schumacher, 3 August, 1926 (15 h.). A brilliant lead by Von Schumacher without prior inspection. Second ascent: H. Tillmann, W. Welzenbach, 14 September, 1929 (9 h., they thought it looked like 5 h.). First British ascent: R. Smith, B. Wakefield, 25-26 July, 1960. Corresp. Bauer-Wakefield, 1960. Rpt. 1978.

53 From the foot of the rib either (a) climb L below it, cross a bergschrund and go up steep straightforward snow into a broad snow gully L of the rib, stonefall likely. Near the top move R up a snow inlet and cross R over icy shelves to the rib crest and continue on its R side. Or less pleasantly but probably sheltered from stonefall (b), just R of the rib toe is a small inlet (bergschrund). Cross it R and climb steep loose rock on R side of crest to approach the crest after 5 rope lengths and a little further up where (a) is joined. Continue up steep friable shale on R side of crest, liberally mixed with snow/ice, with a few short pitches of III to a snowband about one third distance up the rib. The rib above steepens and merges into a rockface R of the continuation rib. Ascend steep snow in the lower rib line to a zone of smooth slabby rock. Now traverse L for a short way across the base of this zone, exposed, IV, to an obvious ice glazed groove. Ascend this awkwardly by mainly slabby pitches for 4 rope lengths, trending somewhat R with bits of IV/IV+, protection poor. At the top of this section a direct ascent on slabs for one 30m.

pitch leads to a crucial traverse L on ice to join the L-hand continuation rib. Continue on the crest over large granite blocks and small pinnacles with good holds. Higher up keep L of the crest until the snow flank at the R side of the upper snow ridge is reached. Climb onto this fine snow/ice crest and follow it to the rock headwall. The crest is longer than it looks and is often thin snow over ice and time consuming. At the top, climb direct for a short pitch up a difficult cracked wall, verglassed (IV+). No proper belay. Get into a glassy gully/groove above (belay) and climb this for another pitch to belay round a corner R (IV/IV+). Go straight up the gully/depression on good rock for 50m. (III+) to the summit cornice and break through this to finish (10-14 h. from foot of rib).

Fiescherwand Direct (Welzenbach Route). The least frequented of Welzenbach's famous series of Bernese north wall climbs, from which it follows that it is the most serious undertaking. The lower part of the rte. is on very rotten rock and the terminal snow/ice section is prone to bad avalanche conditions, apart from the danger of falling séracs which rake all this section. In the context of bad rock the climbing is comparable with the Lauterbrunnen Breithorn, but worse than this rte. as regards objective danger. Some ascents have been made with little evidence of ice and stonefall, but these circumstances are exceptional.

The lower rocky zone is seamed by a series of ribs rising about halfway up the face. Their angle varies little and averages 58°. The icefield above is a fairly broad plain slope in its lower half, about 52° steep; it is cut off almost completely across its breadth by an ever-changing sérac barrier presenting menacing ice cliffs to the slope below. 1200m., TD+ with pitches of IV. First ascent: H. Tillmann, W. Welzenbach, 5 September, 1930 (12½ h.). No British ascent of the original Welzenbach rte. has been made. In winter: M. Dörflinger,

T. Grass, P. Jungen, U. Kämpfer, 9-10 March, 1969. Inclusive of other direct rte. lines on the face (see below),
climbed about 18 times to end of 1977.

54 At the centre foot of the face start below the 4th rib counting
from the R, but excluding the NE rib further R. This rib is
at first more broken than the others and rises towards the
lowest part of the upper icefield. From an avalanche cone,
cross a fairly large bergschrund, normally not difficult, under
the gully between the 3rd and 4th ribs, and ascend diagonally
L on snow/ice to a broken ramp rising L in brittle rock.
Follow this to crest line of 4th rib, and go up its L side for
several rope lengths on rock and ice until it merges into a
sheer slabby section. Now make a long and variable rising
traverse L over rock, ice plaques and ramps below a continuously steep wall above; very delicate and exposed. An
upper ice ramp leads steeply on to the 5th rib. Climb this rib
direct on better rock with good holds and pitches of IV/IV+,
normally with little snow or ice, the most pleasant section of
the climb. At the top reach a small secondary icefield adjoining
the main one, which is higher and to the R. Ascend icefield
diagonally at a low level to R, towards the rock fringe dividing
it from the main icefield; badly exposed to falling rock and
ice. Either take a low rising traverse line R along the top of
the big rock wall of the main face where it joins the higher rock
fringe, ledges and a ramp, or climb above (L of) the first
buttress of the rock fringe and go up ice gullies to the edge of
the main icefield.

Ascend the icefield direct, aiming for the L end of the ice
cliffs somewhat L of the summit line; 8 rope lengths at 52°.
Take a gully/depression under the L side of the cliffs then
trend R on to a ramp formation rising above the cliffs. Follow
this narrowing feature with sustained ice climbing for 5 rope
lengths over one or two small schrunds, and finally trend L
to the NE summit ridge which is followed steeply and thinly

for 50m. to the top (10-15 h. from foot of face).

Other routes on Fiescherwand. The rib bordering the L-hand side of the main face, finishing with a dangerous rising movement R below big ice cliffs supporting the Fiescherhorn plateau, to join the Welzenbach exit only a rope length below the NE summit ridge, was climbed (TD+) by Frln. M. Lüthi with H. Steuri, 1937. The 3rd rib on the lower face was climbed up its R side then ascended diagonally L to a big headwall leading towards the R-hand side of the upper icefield, from where a direct ascent through the middle of the crowning sérac led to the NW ridge about 50m. from the summit (TD+): E. Reiss, A. Reist, H. Sollberger, 1949. Another line between the Welzenbach and 1937 rtes. was climbed (ED-) by S. McCartney, D. Wilkinson, 1977.

OCHS (KLEINES FIESCHERHORN) 3900m.

LK 1249. A beautiful satellite snow and rock peak of the Fiescherhorn group, frequently climbed because of its classic type snow rtes. The peak is invariably ascended from the Grindelwald direction but it is easier from the Finsteraarhorn hut. Generally superlative climbing at a standard on steep gl. terraces and narrow corniced ridges. Its NW face is an extension of the Fiescherwand and is a comparatively safe expedition for north-walling climbers. First ascent: E. von Fellenberg with P. Baumann, P. Inäbnit, P. & U. Kaufmann, 28 July, 1864. In winter: G. A. Hasler with C. Jossi, 20 January, 1902 (same day as Gr. Fiescherhorn).

55 South-West Ridge. This short and normally corniced ridge rises from the large snow plateau under the E and S sides of the Fiescherhörner. It offers the easiest way to the summit from Finsteraarhorn hut, indeed from any direction. PD. Details as for a combination of Rtes. 48 and 51 (5 h. from hut to summit). An alternative way from the snow plateau is to move R up to the Fiescherjoch, Rte. 71 (3694m.) and follow the SE ridge (Rte. 56) to top.

<u>South-East Ridge</u>.　A good introduction for climbers of some experience to the nature of serious snow/ice climbs of the pure variety at the lower end of the difficulty scale.　Arguably one of the best expeditions of its class in the Alps.　Interesting rte. finding problems within narrow, and therefore alternative pitch-type, limits.　The normal rte. from the Strahlegg hut. PD+/AD.

　　The E face of the mtn. is formed by a series of 4 overlapping gl. terraces, which get progressively steeper and more contorted from L (S) to R (N), and each is supported on uneven rock barriers.　Each terrace carries an approach to a fairly large and sloping snowband directly below the final peak.　The terraces are progressively more difficult from L to R.　If the far R-hand one were climbed, so should the face above the sloping snowband be taken direct to a pt. on the ridge just L of the summit, D+.　In fact terraces 3 and 4 are rarely climbed. No. 2 is AD and exposed to falling séracs, but it has been climbed quite often.　The L-hand terrace is the normal way to the snowband under the ridge.　First ascensionists, but No. 1 terrace was first climbed by J. P. Farrar with D. Maquignaz, 1897.

56　From the Strahlegg hut follow a short track on to the gl., which is crossed to the S, to below and L of the rognon capped by pt. 3015. 4m. LK 50.　This is the foot of the 1st gl. terrace. Climb it more or less just R of centre.　At first it is almost an icefall, then the slope eases but there are large crevasses and ice bulges where good rte. finding will avoid deadends and retracing steps.　The terrace is not wide enough for a lot of time to be wasted.　In general keep over to the R, near the edge of the supporting rock barrier in the middle part, but work into the centre again higher up.　Reach a narrow snowband running R with a few crevasses and soon arrive at the foot of

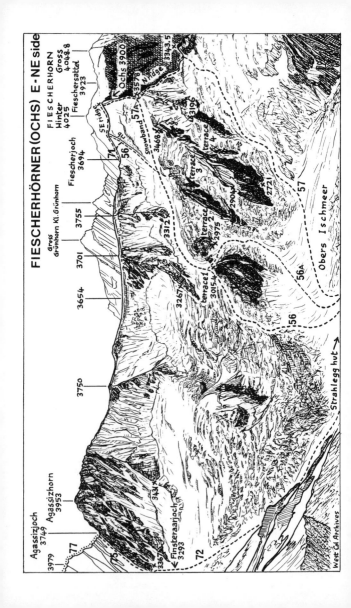

FIESCHERHÖRNER (OCHS) E·NE side

a conspicuous blunt snow rib leading up to a prominent but nameless and unmarked shoulder pt. on the SE ridge. Climb this pleasant rib to the ridge. Beware of cornice on other side. Now follow the narrow and exposed snow/ice ridge, generally corniced and steeper at the top, to the sharp summit, merely a corniced tip ($4\frac{1}{2}$ h. from hut).

It is normal to descend by the same rte. However, one may go down the short airy SW ridge, conditions permitting, and return to the SE ridge by going up to the Fiescherjoch (3694m.). From here do not attempt to descend directly. Go up the ridge to the shoulder top marking the blunt snow rib used in ascent; descend this rib. See Rte. 71.

56A Variation. In the event of the lower part of the 1st terrace being in very bad condition (not uncommon), there is a simple alternative. Cross the gl. and go up the 2nd terrace, immediately R of pt. 3015.4m. Climb on the L, between its icefall and a broken snow slope on the L, just below pt. 2975m., rising to the aforesaid pt. This snow slope spears up into the rock barrier just to the R of pt. 3015.4m. and it can normally be climbed without much trouble to the 1st terrace, above its broken portion. Recommended.

North Ridge. Recommended for a traverse in combination with the previous rte. A very good climb with superb positions and views. The rock parts are actually very loose but normally they are well cemented by snow/ice. Continuously sustained and interesting climbing, but in the event of bad weather below the final section it is an easy matter to traverse off the ridge along the snowband of Rte. 56. AD+. First ascent: E. R. Whitwell with C. Lauener, P. Schlegel, 2 August, 1878.

57 The lowest part of the ridge starts from the Ochsenjoch (3054m.), but it is quicker in good snow conditions to reach the ridge at a higher gap, neither marked nor named on map immediately S of rock peaklet pt. 3343. 5m. From the Strahlegg hut cross the gl. to the SW and climb easy but somewhat crevassed slopes directly towards the aforesaid pt. Turn a few large crevasses at the top, cross a bergschrund and climb a short steep ice slope to the gap on L of the pt. (2 h.). Go up a short snow/rock step in the ridge to a level section which merges into a very steep and broad ice rib, with séracs on the L. Cross a bergschrund and climb a plain slope keeping R, up to a narrowing near some rocks, where another bergschrund may appear. Cross this and climb steep snowy rocks up to the snowcap pt. 3578m., reaching its top by moving L. Cross the snowcap to a broad and almost level snow ridge at the head of the upper snowband on this side of the mtn. Continue to the foot of the steep final section. The crest is usually rocky with a little step in the lower part, but soon continues as a sharp snow ridge at 50-55° with rock on the R, which may require a lot of step cutting. A cornice may form on the R. The last 50m. can be turned by rising up to the L to join the SE ridge just below the sharp summit (4-5 h., 6-7 h. from hut).

57A Variation. A popular shortcut, recommended. The standard remains AD/AD+. From the foot of the blunt snow rib on Rte. 56, make a simple traverse R along the snowband at this level and go up a short steep slope on to the N ridge at the level bit just beyond pt. 3578m. (hut to summit, $5\frac{3}{4}$ h.).

<u>North-West Face.</u> A diamond shaped symmetrical wall directly under the summit, forming a L wing of the Fiescherwand. The wall is divided in 5 parts; a central rock rib rising into a lower oblong icefield whose R side is prominently marked by hanging ice cliffs at 3300m. Above this a lateral rockband then another oblong icefield below a large rock headwall. All these features can be seen clearly on the map. Altogether

this face offers mixed climbing at a high standard with virtually no objective danger. It is steeper than any part of the main Fiescherwand and the climbing is harder and more interesting. At least 3 exits have been taken up the headwall; the way furthest L is just as hard as the others and is taken when more direct lines are badly verglassed. The rock, gneiss, is mostly fair to good, though rather loose in cracks and chimneys at the top. Good holds and stances with easy pegging almost everywhere. Generally recommended by all who have climbed it. 1050m., TD+ with pitches of IV+, average angle 62°. First ascent: Frln. M. Lüthi with H. Steuri, 9 August, 1936 (9 h.). This time has never been bettered and conditions then on the face were bad. Done in nailed boots. First British ascent: R. Milward, S. Parr, July, 1977 (15 h.). Climbed about 11 times to date.

58 The approach is Rte. 52. Start at the foot of the obvious central rock rib directly in the summit line. In some seasons it projects below the bergschrund but at all events its crest is normally reached up steep snow from the R side. Ascend the rib by a series of short steps cut by numerous little snowbands, on loose rock with pitches of II, for 300m. to the first icefield. Go up this directly in the same line, having a natural continuation in a mixed rock/ice rib cutting the 1st icefield zone. It may be easier to keep R of the crest line in this section. Reach the long rockband dividing the 1st and 2nd icefields at a ledge/ramp. Climb diagonally L on ice along base of wall for 2 rope lengths to a gully/depression cutting it. Climb this by a normally difficult ice pitch, then trend R over icy slabs for another pitch (III or harder) into the middle of a rock buttress. Climb this direct with snow/ice to the lower edge of the 2nd icefield. Go up the icefield direct, 53° steep, to its highest pt. in the summit line. There is a large overhanging crack in the lower part of the headwall above, which is 350m. high.

Original finish. Climb 15m. L to a sloping ledge of grit

or snow. This ledge is a conspicuous feature running right across the bottom part of the headwall. Move delicately R on ledge for a few m. Above are small twin pillars. Climb a loose chimney between them up its L side to a large over-hanging chockstone (IV). A through rte. below the chock is taken to easier ground (IV+). Now climb diagonally L for 30m. to another overhang, and go over this direct (IV+) to a smooth slab pitch of 15m. (IV+, icy). Above, easier rocks lead to the large snowband slanting up R below the summit triangle. Cross this snowband trending slightly R (delicate) and climb two good pitches trending R on the wall above which has good holds but some loose rock (III) to the L end of a small snowband slanting up R. Keep straight up the wall on steep slabby rock (IV), trending a little L to reach the N ridge about 2 rope lengths from the top (13-15 h. from foot of face).

Surest but least direct finish. As above, climb 15m. L to a sloping ledge of grit or snow. Follow it L for 3 delicate pitches until the ledge is seen going round a corner. About 10m. before this pt., climb direct for 50m. then trend R (III) to a conspicuous block at the foot of a wet gully slanting L. Take the gully for one pitch and exit by an overhang onto a sloping terrace (IV). Descend L to a narrow ledge and follow this L for a rope length to a snow gully. Climb the bed for a rope length or use slabs on R (III). Continue diagonally L to a shoulder in another rope length. The next pitch is taken direct over 3 overhangs to reach a narrow ledge with a stance further R (IV+). Above the stance another direct pitch with an overhang attains a better snowy ledge (IV), at the L end of the snowband rising R under the summit triangle. Continue direct for a long pitch to reach the N ridge where sustained ice or mixed climbing leads in 4 rope lengths to the summit.

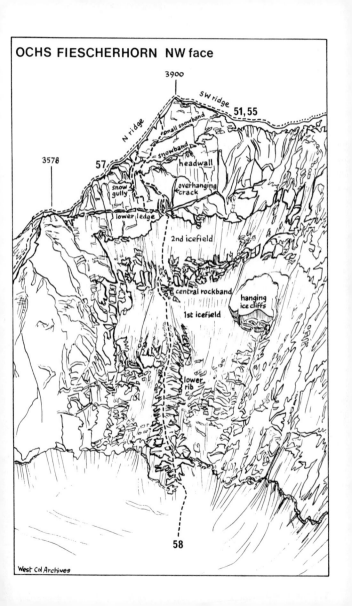

GROSS GRÜNHORN   4043.5m.

KLEIN GRÜNHORN   3913m.

GRÜNEGGHORN   3860m.

LK 1249.   After the Fiescherhorn, the principal summits on
the ridge running S towards Konkordia. They are comparatively
neglected but the main peak always has a following, being a
four-thousander and finer than many one could name.   The
approach slopes are often badly crevassed but ways can usually
be found round them without wasting too much time.   The ridge
rocks are good everywhere.   West Col Archives Memoir 2704.
First ascent of Gr: E. von Fellenberg with P. Egger, P. Inäbnit, P. Michel, 7 August 1865. It seems that the peak was not
climbed again by the same ordinary rte. until 1886.   Kl: G.
Lammer, A. Lorria, 13 August, 1885.   Grünegghorn: probably
G. A. Hasler with P. Bernet, 26 September, 1903 (AJ 21, 562).
Winter ascents, etc.   Details fail.

Gr. Grünhorn Normal Route.   The easiest and shortest way,
bad crevasses possible.   F+.   First ascensionists.

59 From Konkordia hut go up the R side of the Ewigschneefeld
beside its icefall, crevasses, to just beyond pt. 3135m.   Now
ascend R up the broad gl. band to NE, numerous crevasses.
Higher up work to the E, going up a badly crevassed zone to a
col (not marked on map, but obvious) between the Gr. Grünhorn
and Grünegghorn ($3\frac{3}{4}$ h.).   Now ascend the SW ridge of the
mtn., keeping a little on its L side (45 min., $4\frac{1}{2}$ h. from hut).

By traverse of Grünegghorn.   Less crevassed than the normal
rte.   F+/PD-.

60 From Konkordia hut go up the Grüneggfirn then slant N up
snow slopes leading directly to the secondary peak.   Keep L
and climb the first snow funnel in the rocks of the L-hand (SW)
ridge, which opens to the R (N) of pt. 3475m.   Go up through
this funnel on to the ridge and follow it easily on snow to
pt. 3787m.   Continue along a narrow rock crest to the Grünegghorn summit (4 h.).   Descend easy rocks in a few min. to

the col at the foot of the SW ridge of the parent mtn. where Rte. 59 is joined (1 h., 5 h. from hut).

Traverse with Kl. Grünhorn. A fine expedition, rarely done, but unreservedly recommended in combination with a descent over the Grünegghorn (R. G. C. with June Ross, 13 August, 1956). PD+. The N ridge section of the Gr. is the key part, on good rock with short pitches of III. N ridge: J. P. Farrar, H. V. Reade, 4 August, 1907. Without Kl., traverse by N ridge and Grünegghorn: O. K. Williamson with H. Fux and a porter, 6 July, 1921.

61 Go up the Ewigschneefeld as for Rte. 59 but keep more to the L up the broad gl. band, passing below the W face of the Gr. Continue in the same direction (NE) and reach the SW ridge of the Kl. which is climbed on snow to its final rock part and the summit. PD- (4 h.). Descend the pleasant rock ridge towards the Gr., turning one step on the R before reaching the foot of the Gr. N ridge. After an easy section the ridge rises in a big step to the summit. An initial wall is climbed by moving slightly L of the crest. Continue near the crest then work R and cross a couloir and a wall beyond to reach a rib, facing W, which leads back to the ridge. (This part of the step has been climbed in favourable conditions on the more icy L side of crest). Now go straight up a series of short, steep, delicate pitches, awkward when snow covered; except for moving a little to the R in one or two places, stay on the crest and so reach the summit. Pitches of III (4 h., 8 h. from hut). Now reverse Rte. 60 over the Grünegghorn.

62 By South-East Ridge of Grünegghorn. A frequented approach from the Finsteraarhorn hut. From the Grünhornlücke ascend snow to the rocks of the Grünhörnli, which are mounted from their upper L side near the bottom of the ridge. By a broken gully reach the crest and follow this pleasantly to the

Grünhörnli (3594. 4m.).   Continue by a short snow then narrow craggy ridge with several short steps and gendarmes in good rock, finally by an airy mixed section up to the Grünegghorn where Rte. 60 is joined (4 h. , plus 1 h. more to Gr. Grünhorn). PD+. Recommended.

<u>South-East Face</u>.   The classic direct summit rte. from the Finsteraarhorn hut, recommended when conditions are good. PD+/AD. First ascent: E. Schiess and party, 1913.

63 From the Finsteraarhorn hut cross the gl. towards the Grünhornlücke and go into the large snow bay under the SE face. On the R a steep snow couloir splits the rock wall of pt. 3585m. Climb it to the snow ridge above which is followed over a bulge till it merges into the face. Climb a steep snow slope and go up mixed terrain above, interesting with good rock, keeping fairly close to the edge of the E face on your R. Climb direct to the summit (5 h. from hut).

64 <u>East Pillar</u>.   A fine climb on mostly good rock and short difficulties on ice. 650m. , D with a pitch of IV+ and V. First ascent: C. Blum, U. Frei, 27 July, 1967 (10 h.). In winter: P. Etter, U. Gantenbein, R. Käser, A. Scherrer, 10 January, 1973 ($7\frac{1}{2}$ h.).

From the Finsteraarhorn hut go to the foot of the rte. in $1\frac{1}{2}$ h. Start from a gl. terrace about 150m. R of pt. 3325m. Cross a bergschrund and climb a short snow/ice slope to rocks L of a shallow couloir coming down from the foot of the L edge of a large triangular pillar/buttress. Go all the way up a rib on the L side of this couloir for 300m. with numerous slab pitches then short steps and little towers, finishing up a chimney on a snowband under a rock wall (pitches of III and IV). Traverse R on snow/ice above the lower couloir to the inner flank of the pillar/buttress, now well above its base. Climb this trending R near the R-hand edge, a pitch of IV, then a loose section over big blocks, followed by a gully pitch into an exposed gap. Above this a step of 30m. (V) is followed by a pitch of IV+, then pitches of III to the top of the pillar/buttress. About 150m. in all from entry traverse. Move L along its short sharp crest, awkward, to foot of next pillar step. Make a rising traverse L to reach a gully and follow this to top of step (III). Reach a narrow ledge system below the upper pillar/buttress. In the base of this climb a fault slanting steeply L over slabs to a corner and shallow gully leading straight up to the pillar crest above the upper buttress. Follow L side of crest for a short way, then climb an obvious depression by a rising traverse L, then R, to go over the edge forming the SE face. So reach the last rocks of Rte. 63 and climb these easily to summit (6-8 h. from bergschrund).

65 Kl. Grünhorn East Wall Rib. Another fine, sound rock climb, following the obvious rib descending from the summit. AD+ with pitches of II, III and IV/IV+. 400m. First ascent: C. Blum, U. Frei, 24 July, 1967 (4 h.). Approach from Finsteraarhorn hut in 2 h. Above a bergschrund, go up rib direct to below the summit step (pitches of II, III). A small chimney/ gully, deep in places, leads up the E facing wall to a small stance on R flanking edge. Traverse R for a few m., then go up direct on vertical rock (IV/IV+) to reach the rib crest again and finish up this briefly to summit (4 h. from bergschrund).

GRÜNHORNLÜCKE 3286m.

LK 1249. Between the Grünegghorn and (Wyssnollen) Fiescher Gabelhorn. A well trodden and easy gl. pass. See Rte. 9. First crossing: R. Meyer with A. Abbühl, J. Bortis, K. Huber, A. Volker, 17 August, 1812.

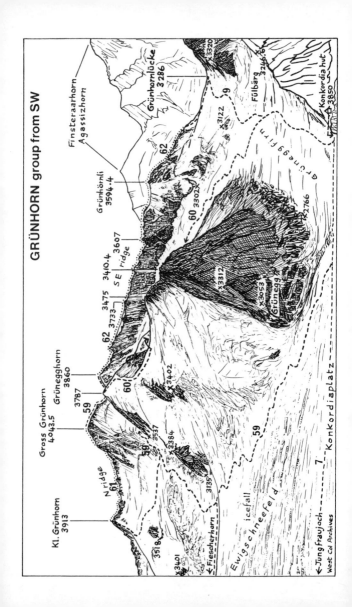

GRÜNHORN group from SW

FIESCHER GABELHORN   3875.8m.

66 LK 1249. Rarely climbed. This summit is a large double rock pinnacle, rather poor granite and gneiss. Reached in $3\frac{1}{2}$ h. from Finsteraarhorn hut by obvious rte. up the NE ridge (PD), or easily from the Gabelhornsattel (3765m.) and the SE ridge. Badly crevassed slopes. The W rock ridge from Kamm is AD. First ascent: P. and C. Montandon, 8 August, 1889. In winter (on ski): H. Lauper, H. Rüfenacht, 24 March, 1920.

KAMM   3866m.

67 LK 1249. Chamm. A large hoof-like rock peak with precipitous faces on the long ridge running W from the Fiescher Gabelhorn. Some of the rock is quite good (granite). Invariably climbed from Konkordia hut by ridges above and to the E of the Faulberg cwm, track from hut, finishing up a small hanging gl. under the summit. There are many short and interesting quality rock climbs on the Faulberg (Fülbärg, 3242.6m.) immediately behind the Konkordia hut. Grade II and III, or harder. First ascent of Kamm: G. Lammer, A. Lorria, 17 August, 1885.

SCHÖNBÜHLHORN   3854m.

68 LK 1249. Easily climbed by its NW ridge from the Gabelhornsattel (3765m.), $4\frac{3}{4}$ h. from Finsteraarhorn hut. Badly crevassed slopes. First ascent: L. Kurz, A. Barbey with two others, 13 July, 1884.

GROSS WANNENHORN   3905.9m.

LK 1249. A large mtn. almost exclusively snow climbing. Approaches from the S/SW involve some rock climbing. The usual approach from the Finsteraarhorn hut crosses long crevassed slopes. First ascent: G. Studer, R. Lindt with K. Blatter, P. Sulzer, 6 August, 1864.   In winter (on ski): P. Trümpler, K. Steiner, 21 January, 1910.

North-East Flank and East Ridge. The normal and easiest rte., quite pleasant in good snow conditions but tedious with

93

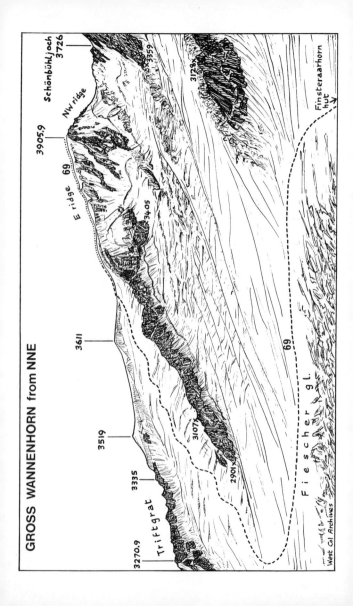

GROSS WANNENHORN from NNE

Schönbühljoch
3726

NW ridge

3905.9

E ridge 69

3405

3359

3128x

3611

3519

3335

Triftgrat

3270.9

3107x

2901x

Finsteraarhorn
hut

69

Fiescher gl.

69

West Col Archives

bad snow. F+. First ascensionists.

69 From the Finsteraarhorn hut cross the gl. SSE, keeping
straight across until a broken section at 2950m. is turned. On
the opposite side descend until you are below pt. 2901m., then
go up the crevassed gl. cwm to the S. The best line up the
cwm depends on the disposition of crevasses; sometimes take
the middle, other times it is better to keep R, near the long
rock escarpment marking the R side of the cwm. Either way,
near the top keep R of and below snow hump pt. 3611m., then
reach the E ridge on the R. Follow this or its broad flank L
(cornice on R) to the summit rocks (4 h. from hut).

KLEIN WANNENHORN 3706.7m.

70 LK 1249. This peak has excellent climbing on granite.
There is a steep classic rte. up the SE face (IV): W. Baumgartner, W. Diehl, 15 July, 1935. The S ridge is II/III and
the long ESE (Distelgrat) ridge is II/III, and can be done in
two sections - the lower part finishing in a gap after pt. 3154m.
Popular with local Swiss climbers. The easiest descents are
crevassed snow slopes. There is a specially prepared and
comfortable bivouac place for these climbs at pt. 2028.6m.
near the Flesch tarn. See Rte. 10.
   First ascent: W. H. Gladstone, C. S. Parker, S. Taylor with
F. Schwick, J. Tännler, 23 August, 1866.

FIESCHERJOCH 3694m.

71 LK 1249. Marked but not named on map, a slight col at
the foot of the SE ridge of Ochs. Today only used by parties
doing a circuit of the Fiescherhörner peaks and wanting to
return to the Strahlegg hut side.   For moving between the
Strahlegg hut and Finsteraarhorn hut it is more usual to use
the Finsteraarjoch/Agassizjoch combination.   The col is a
narrow, corniced snow saddle and its NE side is not ascended/
descended directly.   The blunt rib of Rte. 56 is taken to $\frac{3}{4}$ height
(in ascent) then a traverse L on moderately steep snow to the
SE ridge of Ochs, followed by a short descent to the saddle,
PD+. The SW side is a 50m. snow slope above the Fiescherhörner plateau.   See also comments in Rtes. 55, 56.   First

crossing: Leslie Stephen and a large party, 1862.

FINSTERAARJOCH 3293m.

LK 1249, 1250. Between the Agassizhorn and pt. 3468.7m. of the Strahlhörner. A fine gl. passage with exceptional views and scenery, one of the grandest in the Bernese Alps, generally used today as an approach to important climbs. Both sides PD/AD according to conditions found on the gls., normally broken and very crevassed. Parties wishing to go from the Strahlegg hut to Lauteraar hut will probably find the Strahlegg-pass more straightforward. First recorded crossing: H. B. George with C. Almer, 28 July, 1862. On ski: R. Helbling, A. Pellaud, 29 January, 1903. In winter without ski: A. W. Moore, H. Walker with C. Almer, M. Anderegg, P. Bohren, 23 December, 1866 (returned over Strahleggpass without stopping). Winter traverse complete: W. A. Moore (no relation!) and party, 12 January, 1932.

72 From the Strahlegg hut a small track makes a rising traverse over moraine or snow then rocks beside pt. 2750m. to the SE, above the gl., to the snowfield near pt. 2919m. When in doubt on this section, keep rising L. There are now two ways. Either pass between the rock toe ahead along a snowband, pt. 2922m., with a slabby rock island lower down, and continue traversing horizontally to pass immediately below rock rognon 3013m. (LK 50), thereafter rising L under its rocks to a higher level on the gl. Or take a higher traverse line across the first rock toe, at a break well shown on map, and continue the traverse on snow to pass above rognon 3013m. The latter is longer but less crevassed; the former can be quite complicated. Now continue rising gradually up the gl. slopes to a crevassed zone in the same S direction. Pass above or below this according to conditions, to reach the upper snowfield, still with long crevasses. Keep L to avoid crevasses, coasting under pt. 3468.7m. to reach the broad saddle (3-3$\frac{1}{2}$ h.).

73 From the Lauteraar hut follow Rte. 14 to the corner before

96

the Aar Biv. hut ($1\frac{1}{4}$ h.). Directly ahead (SW) is the Finster icefall. Move L (S) and pass close to pt. 2668m., to turn the icefall on this side, then bear R over a flat section away from the foot of the Studerhorn N face. This section can be very complicated. Later return gradually L (W) and turn the second icefall section by passing fairly close to pt. 3199m. LK 50 (just below pt. 3277m.), at the foot of the NE rib of the Finsteraarhorn. Continue close to the foot of this mtn., turning a crevassed boss on the R, and so reach the easy upper plateau which is crossed directly to the saddle (4-5 h., 6 h. from Lauteraar hut, 1 h. shorter from Aar biv.).

AGASSIZHORN   3953m.

LK 1249. A little imitator of the Finsteraarhorn (Hasler). A handsome snow and rock peak somewhat dominated by its mighty neighbour. A worthwhile climb and outstanding viewpoint. It is the one peak which is both visible from Grindelwald and the Grimsel Hospice. First ascent: W. A. B. Coolidge with U. Almer, C. Inäbnit, 7 September, 1872. In winter: A. Fischer with U. Almer, 3 January, 1896. On ski: H. C. H. Dowding, A. Lunn, F. L. Robinson with J. Knubel, J. Bischoff, 22 April, 1903.

<u>South-South-East Flank</u>.   A pleasant snow outing, F+. First ascensionists.

74 From the Agassizjoch (see below) climb the broad snow flank of the ridge to the summit (30 min., 3 h. from Finsteraarhorn hut). Starting from this hut it is not necessary to go right up to the pass; bear L and climb the S flank at its easiest pt. to the summit ($2\frac{3}{4}$ h.).

AGASSIZJOCH   3749m.

LK 1249. Between the Agassizhorn and Finsteraarhorn, the usual passage from the Strahlegg hut to the Finsteraarhorn

hut, and an access rte. to both mtns. An impressive outing.
The W side is F+. The E side is a big 350m. high couloir of
the classic type, somewhat exposed to stonefall and liable to
avalanche in bad conditions. A lot of sweat has been poured
into this place but it is a trade rte. of a kind, PD+. First
crossing: J. J. Hornby, F. Morshead, T. H. Philpott with
C. Almer, J. Anderegg, C. Lauener, 7 August, 1866. Couloir
side in winter: nameless Englishman with C. Jossi, J. Kaufmann, 16 January, 1889.

75 From the Strahlegg hut follow Rte. 72 to the Finsteraarjoch
$(3-3\frac{1}{2}$ h.). By traversing the snow plateau close below the
Agassizhorn, reach the foot of the couloir without losing height.
Cross a bergschrund and climb the R side of the snow/ice slope
which averages 45° but is slightly steeper at the top. Except
in good snow conditions (crampons) after a cold night, climb
rocks on the R side as soon as possible. Move onto a loose
rock rib which can be followed all the way up. At the top,
when almost level with the col, traverse L across an inter-
vening groove and rib on to the final slope and so reach the col
$(2-3$ h., $5-6\frac{1}{2}$ h. from Strahlegg hut). An afternoon descent
is compulsory if returning from the Finsteraarhorn to the
Strahlegg hut.

76 From the Finsteraarhorn hut descend to the gl. and go up
the simple gl. slope below a long rock barrier coming down
from the col. Two sections broken by crevasses. Climb the
slope keeping R to the pass $(2\frac{1}{2}$ h.).

FINSTERAARHORN   4273.9m.

LK 1249. Monarch of the Bernese Alps. A magnificent and
almost symmetrical, fin-like rock pile, dark in colour, standing at the head of one of the largest and most remote gl. systems
in the Alps. Originally known on the Valais side as Schwarzhorn, and first publicised with remarkable accuracy by its
present name in 1789 through Coxe's 'Travels in Switzerland'.
It has an early and complex climbing history, and the first

ascent has been disputed with long and erudite arguments in Alpine literature. The ordinary rte. from the Finsteraarhorn hut is quite short, but climbs from other huts are long and often much more difficult. The rock is fair to good on the ridges. A very popular mtn. West Col Archives Memoir 2682.

First ascent (by SE ridge reached from the Studerfirn): A. Abbühl, J. Bortis, A. Volker, 16 August, 1812, the guides of the Meyer family. 2nd ascent: J. Leuthold, J. Währen, 10 August, 1829, supported by Hugi and sometimes quoted as the first ascent by the anti-Meyer faction. By a tourist (4th): J. Sulger with A. Abplanalp, J. Jaun, H. Lorentz, 6 September, 1842. By a British party in 1857. In winter: E. Boss, U. Almer, 8 March, 1887. On ski: H. Hoek with G. Moor, A. Tännler, 11 November, 1901.

North-West (Agassiz) Ridge. The normal rte. for parties coming from the Grindelwald side. A long and somewhat tiring climb, half rock, half snow/ice. PD, but PD+ to col. First ascent: G. E. Foster with H. Baumann, P. Bernet, 28 July, 1868.

77 From the Strahlegg hut follow Rtes. 72, 75 to the Finsteraarjoch and Agassizjoch (5-6$\frac{1}{2}$ h.). Above the col, climb the snow and rock ridge to its steep and loose upper section. Stay on the exposed crest and reach pt. 3979m. (1$\frac{1}{4}$ h.). Cross the flattish slope ahead, corniced on L, to the mainly snowy step rising to the Hugisattel. This has short rockbands at the bottom and top. Climb in a curve to the R, returning L, up steep snow or ice and reach the rock outcrop crest of the saddle above (4088m.) (30 min. - 1$\frac{1}{4}$ h.). Cross the Hugisattel and climb the final pleasant ridge, mainly rock, on its crest (1 h., 2$\frac{3}{4}$-3$\frac{1}{2}$ h. from Agassizjoch, 8-10 h. from Strahlegg hut).

South-West Flank and North-West Ridge. The ordinary rte. and the easiest rte. on the mtn. A pleasant outing. F+/PD-. Second ascensionists.

78 From the Finsteraarhorn hut climb a steep snow slope on the L side of the rock island on which the hut stands, up to near pt. 3231.3m. Climb the snow slopes above (N), and once

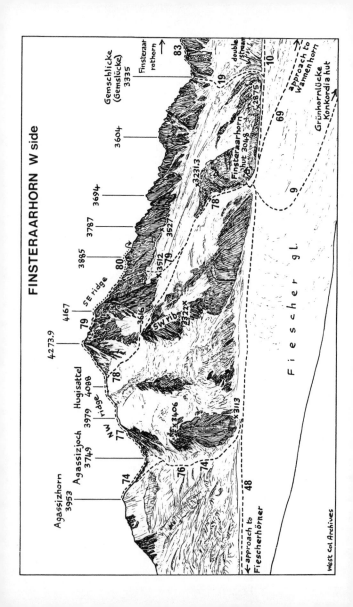

FINSTERAARHORN W side

Agassizhorn 3953

Agassizjoch 3749

Hugisattel 4088

3979 NW ridge 77

78 4273.9

SE ridge 79

4167

3885

3787 3694

3604

Gemschlücke (Gemslücke) 3335

Finsteraarhorn 83

double stream

19

10

approach to Wännenhorn

69

2875

Finsteraarhorn hut 3048

6

78

9

Grünhornlücke Konkordia hut

3604

3787

3694

3527

79

x3512

80

366

SW rib

3322x

3231.3

Fiescher gl.

74

76

3406

74

x3113

48

← approach to Fiescherhörner

West Col Archives

above the level of the last rock outcrop on L, traverse L to some rocks and go up to a low relief saddle slightly above pt. 3616m. in the SW rib of the mtn. The breakfast place. Pass through to the other side and climb an easy slope, crevasses, to the Hugisattel (2½ h.). Now go up the final part of the NW ridge as for the previous rte. (1 h., 3½ h. from hut).

South-East Ridge. This long ridge starts from the Gemslücke (3335m.). Its middle and upper sections carry three notable but small towers. The ridge supplies the classic rte. up the mtn., and starting from the Finsteraarhorn hut it can be reached by climbing the flank at several points. Only the usual approach to the ridge is described; recommended for making a traverse of the mtn. PD+ with short pitches of III. First ascent by this approach: G.H. Morse with H. & U. Almer, 4 August, 1887.

79 From the Finsteraarhorn hut follow Rte. 78 to above pt. 3231.3m. Climb snow slopes to the NE and go into the snow bay on the R of the big rock spur descending to pt. 3512m. At the top of this bay and about 200m. to R of the spur are two parallel couloirs in the side of the ridge. Bergschrund. Climb a pleasant red rock rib (II) dividing the couloirs, easily seen on map, to the ridge above, reached at a pt. well above the last tower, pt. 3885m. Follow the pleasantly exposed ridge to pt. 4167m. Continue along the sharp, shattered crest with interest and good rock over little pinnacles to below the summit step of 40m. Traverse and descend slightly over little ribs to reach a short, smooth recessed slab. Cross this (III), often icy, fixed rope, to a chimney/gully immediately L, and climb this up its L edge (III, fixed rope) to a short rib leading to the summit (4½-5½ h. from hut). Direct ascent of 40m. step is IV+.

South-East Ridge from Studerfirn. This is the easiest of the

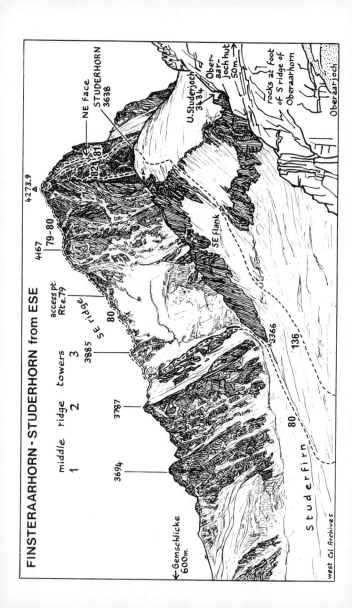

FINSTERAARHORN - STUDERHORN from ESE

middle ridge towers
1 2 3

Gemschlicke 600m.

3694

3787

3885
SE ridge

80

access pt.
Rte.79

4467

79-80

4273.9

82 81

NE face
STUDERHORN
3638

U.Studerjoch 3434

Ober-
aar-
joch hut
50m.

rocks at foot
of S ridge of
Oberaarhorn

Oberaarjoch

3366

136

80

SE flank

Studerfirn

west Cal Archives

direct ways from the Oberaarjoch hut. Climbed infrequently. Reaching the crest constitutes the main difficulty. This can be done in a number of ways by lines which are close to each other, but the one normally easiest is described. AD-/AD. First ascensionists. (The easiest rte. from the Oberaarjoch hut is to cross the Gemslücke, Rte. 19, and make a long traverse over snow slopes to reach the rib of Rte. 79. This approach, PD. About 7 h.).

80 From the Oberaarjoch hut climb the centre of the easy Studerfirn into its NW corner, below a hanging gl. to the L of pt. 4167m. on the ridge above (falling ice) ($1\frac{1}{2}$ h.). On the L of the hanging gl. slope, at its top, is the 3rd ridge tower (3885m.). Immediately L of this is a snowy rock rib, narrow but pronounced, which lies in an otherwise icy slope and descends to the L hand side of the icefall base of the gl. slope. Cross the bergschrund, sometimes quite difficult, and climb the rib on loose rocks. If the bergschrund is impossible, a somewhat risky traverse on to the rib can be made from the actual foot of the icefall slope. The rib is also exposed to stonefall. Reach the ridge ($2\frac{1}{4}$ h.) and continue along the crest over pt. 3885m., narrow and corniced, followed by similar work to where the Finsteraarhorn hut rte. reaches the ridge. Continue as for this rte. to the top ($2\frac{3}{4}$ h., $6\frac{1}{2}$ h. from Oberaarjoch hut).

North-East Rib. The NE face of the mtn. is one of the most impressive in the Bernese Alps. It is 1050m. high, in a remote situation and few parties have climbed it. It was the first of the classic N walls in the Alps to be climbed and has had the least publicity. The face has a prominent rib running down its centre, with a base pt. 3199m. on LK 50, omitted on LK 25 which instead marks the top of an initial splayed out step on the rib, with twin toes, as pt. 3277m. A companion parallel rib, not altogether continuous, lies to the L (E). This

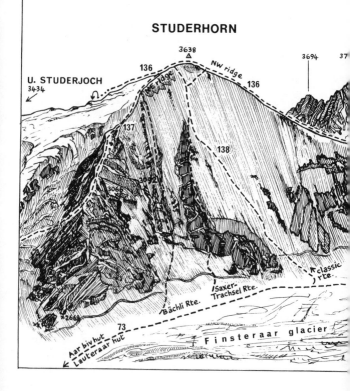

from NE

STUDERHORN

3638 △

NW ridge

3694   37

U. STUDERJOCH
3434

136

136

3396

137

138

3066

3694   37

classic
rte.

Saxer-
Trachsel Rte.

Bächli Rte.

2669

Aar biv hut
Lauteraar hut

73

Finsteraar glacier

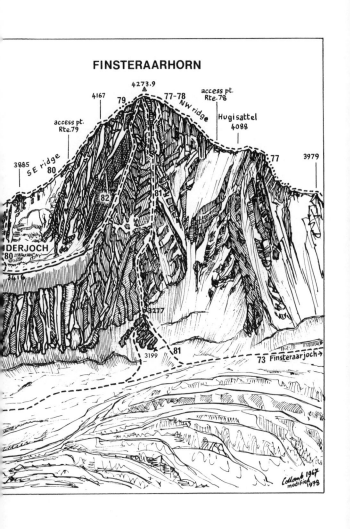

FINSTERAARHORN

is the E rib, the upper part of which is a separate climb (see below). The two ribs are divided by a huge couloir system, ordinarily a rubbish chute and very exposed to stonefall. Whereas parts of the NE rib are pronounced and resemble a ridge, other sections, notably near the top, flatten into wall-like characteristics. There is no precise rte. up the first 800m. of the rib. Variable lines and pitches are possible according to conditions found - largely a question of avoiding variable amounts of snow/ice on the rocks. Much more serious is the rotten nature of the rock, which deteriorates as height is gained, but with occasional sound pitches, and consequential stonefall. Relatively slight movements on to the rib flanks, always necessary but variable, are exposed to stonefall, and the headwall pitches by any exit remain dangerous in this respect.

The first party to try the ridge (Miss G. L. Bell with H. & U. Fuhrer, 31 July, 1902) retreated in bad weather from near the base of the Grey Tower, were constantly threatened by stonefall and survived two bivouacs. Miraculously, the first ascensionists experienced no stonefall anywhere on the climb. Most subsequent parties have reported serious stonefall.

Comments about the climb - "Owes its difficulty entirely to the looseness and rottenness of the rock ... and because of the objective danger from falling stones, the climb (is) un-justifiable" (O'Brien). "For over 100m. from the traverse (one of the upper pitches) ... was just flirting with death" (Adolf Rubi). "Amatter crawling up those slabs ... seemed to really extend him ... he had for once in his life to climb all out" (Hasler).

A cold-blooded assessment of this rte., ignoring its dangers, puts most of the climbing at II and III, with continuous pitches of IV, but not harder, above the Grey Tower. The accepted overall grade is TD (not TD+). The approach is now much shortened and simplified by the Aar Biv. hut.

First ascent: G. A. Hasler with F. Amatter, 16 July, 1904 (15 h.). Second: H. Bruederlin, V. A. Fynn, 12-14 August, 1906. Third: Miss M. E. O'Brien (American) with A. & F. Rubi, 3 September, 1930 (13 h.), by R-hand exit. First British (5th) ascent: J. O. Talbot with M. Epp, 29 July, 1964, by a traverse from the Studerfirn across the E rib and the dividing couloir on to NE rib. In winter: P. Etter, U. Gantenbein, A. & E. Scherrer, 21-22 December, 1970. Climbed 11 times to end of 1977.

81 From the Aar biv. join Rte. 73 and go up the Finster icefall to foot of rib (2 h.). It is normally best to traverse on to the rib at the top (3277m.) of its first splayed out step. Above the bergschrund this traverse rises diagonally L across ice at 50°. Follow crest of rib, quite easy for at least 300m., by a succession of slabby gully pitches; these are sometimes just L of crest, one or two on the R. Stay on the crest as far as possible, the number of steps increasing higher up (II, III, a few IV) until a smooth zone, normally becoming icy, abuts the Grey Tower about 180m. from the top. This is 25m. high and has never been climbed direct.

L hand Amatter exit. Descend at 45° for 15m. down smooth slabs into a gully groove. This is normally very icy and a further descending traverse L may be necessary before it is possible to resume climbing. Ideally go up the smooth slabs just L of the gully groove and cross it higher up to rejoin rib above the Grey Tower. Continue up the ill defined rib with sustained climbing on poor rock, over several short steps, nearly vertical, trending slightly L to easier ground and exit on the SE ridge 5 min. L of summit. From the upper part of the slabby gully L of the Grey Tower, an exit has been made trending L up a continuation gully followed by at least two dangerous pitches on a steep headwall to reach the SE ridge at much the same place (15-20 h. from foot of rib).

R hand Rubi exit. From foot of Grey Tower make a steep

flanking movement R to reach a vague ledge line above the level of top of tower, running R. Go along this precariously for 30m., then climb steep chimney/groove pitches to the NW ridge which is reached a few min. R of summit. This exit has the doubtful advantage of being more broken and despite the N face aspect possibly less verglassed, but the rock is worse than the L hand exit. The choice of exit is dictated entirely by prevailing conditions, and to date the exits have been climbed roughly an equal number of times.

East Rib. See preamble to previous rte. This rib is the antithesis of the NE one, having little objective danger and mostly excellent rock. The approach is an easy walk up the Studerfirn. The lower section of the rib corresponds with the ascent line to the Ob. Studerjoch; this is loose, unpleasant and even more dangerous than the NE rib, with a menacing sérac wall to contend with at the top. So it does not form part of the climb. The middle and upper ribs are taken from the Studerfirn, the two being joined by a L-ward movement at the level of the Grey Tower on the NE rib. At this pt. the two rtes. are only 75m. apart. A magnificent rock climb, recommended. With fresh snow on the face difficulties mount rapidly and the grading applies only to good conditions. 850m., D+ with pitches of IV+ in 4 sustained sections. First ascent: O. Brügger, H. Kohler, H. Winterberger, 29 September, 1929 ($7\frac{1}{2}$ h.). No information about probable number of ascents.

82 From the Oberaarjoch hut to foot of climb, about $1\frac{3}{4}$ h. From the Ob. Studerjoch (3416m.) go up the last snow slope, cross a small bergschrund and climb to the foot of a deep couloir on the L of an obvious crack. The couloir descends from a small saddle to the L of the first big gendarme on the rib above. Climb into the couloir but quit it as soon as possible, either to the L or R. The rocks on R are sound but more difficult; those on L are loose but easy. Climb to the saddle.

This initial section is quite exposed to stonefall, but thereafter the climbing is mostly safe.

Follow the rib over a succession of gendarmes which are climbed direct on the crest. Reach an unclimbable tower of shiny rock which is turned L by a dièdre/crack (jamming). Higher up the rib merges into the face at a break in the steepness. The continuation rib lies to the L, which at a rather higher level than the pt. reached has a pointed gendarme on its crest. Make a rising traverse L over comparatively easy rocks and snow until level with the gap on R of this gendarme. The face becomes a snow/ice slope with outcrops. Traverse from rock to rock across the face and reach the gap by a narrow verglassed scoop. The rib continues with characteristic gendarmes which can be climbed direct (hard) in good conditions or turned on the L. Reach the SE ridge about 5 min. L of the summit (8-10 h. from bergschrund).

FINSTERAARROTHORN 3530.1m.

83 LK 1249. At the end of the long SE ridge of the Finsteraarhorn. Easily climbed from the Gemslücke (Rte. 19) by the NW ridge in 45 min. F+ ($2\frac{1}{4}$-$2\frac{1}{2}$ h. from Finsteraarhorn hut, 2 h. from Oberaarjoch hut). First ascent: S. Simon, E. Merian with J. Tischhauser, 27 or 31 July, 1885. In winter on ski: K. Steiner, P. Trümpler, 3 January, 1908.

Schreckhorn – Lauteraarhorn chain

METTENBERG   3104.3m.

LK 1229. Mättenberg. A massive rock pile with picturesque precipices, overlooking Grindelwald.   A mixture of gneiss (above 2400m.) and calcareous rock. Reserved for training climbs, but not in fact climbed often. The approaches are tedious. Superb regional view. First ascent: before 1817 by F. Lehmann and a chamois hunter.

<u>South-West Flank (Langer Jahn)</u>. The normal rte., PD. Laborious with a better finish.

84 From the Stieregg inn (1650m.), Rte. 11, a track crosses grass and rocks NW to cross a low rock barrier and enter the Langer Jahn (Lenge Jan) ravine. Climb in the steep bed over sheep pastures and debris, and pass a spring. The upper part consists of easy broken rocks with old snow. At the top reach a headwall, trend L up scree and steep rock shelves into a gully leading directly to the summit.   Alternatively, from below the headwall climb a steep gully trending R to the main ridge SE of the summit and follow this to top ($4\frac{1}{2}$ h.).

Better still, at the foot of the final section of the ravine, trend L up steep rocks on to the SW ridge and climb this with interest (III) to the summit.

ANKENBÄLLI   3164m.

LK 1229.   Fairly prominent ridge pt. after the Mettenberg. No special interest.

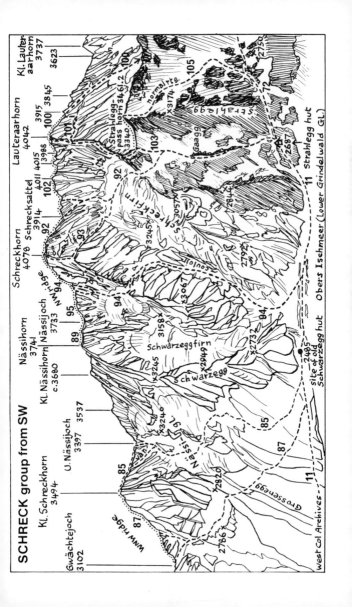

SCHRECK group from SW

GWÄCHTEN 3164m.

LK 1229. Gwächta. Improperly called Gwächtenhorn in some Alpine literature. Similar ridge pt. to Ankenbälli and of identical height.

KLEIN SCHRECKHORN 3494m.

LK 1229. A splendid and frequented training peak and an alternative to its big brother when that mtn. is not in condition. The rock is gneiss and mostly good. First ascent: E. Anderson with C. Almer, P. Bohren, 7 August, 1857. In winter: G. A. Hasler with C. Jossi, early 1904. On ski: A. Lunn with F. Amatter, P. Bernet, 23 April, 1922.

<u>South-East Ridge (from U. Nässijoch).</u> The ridge is quite short above the col (3397m.). The usual rte. to the summit from both hut approaches. PD/PD+. The grade has gone up because of the bad state of the gls. and icy slopes where snow was formerly prevalent. First ascent: Miss M. C. Brevoort, W. A. B. Coolidge with C. & U. Almer, 4 June, 1875.

85 From the Strahlegg hut descend the valley path to the site of the old Schwarzegg hut (2485m.), 45 min. Continue a short way then climb rocks and snow N, on the R side of a moraine, up to the Nässi gl. This is formed in two elongated tiers with a dividing rockband. Reach the gl. at its extreme R side and make a rising traverse L, above an ice cliff, to the foot of the dividing rocks. Broken, icy conditions are common in late season. Continue to the L, sometimes awkward, and go up the lower (W) branch of the gl., crevassed, then take a few rocks and a couloir on the R to reach the col (3397m.) ($3\frac{1}{2}$ h.). A pleasant scramble on the ridge leads to summit (30 min., $4\frac{3}{4}$ h. from Strahlegg hut).

86 From the Gleckstein hut a small track contours grass and rock slopes E, crossing several gullies, rising slightly to below the barriers supporting the Krinnen gl. This traverse line crosses the Bos Bergligraben ravine not far below its head (2620m.). On the other side, after a short descent, continue in the same line, difficult to follow in the dark, under pt. 2700m. and above pt. 2463m., now due S. Skirt or cross old snowbeds, then another short descent round a rock wall is followed by climbing scree and moraine to some barriers. Up to the L these barriers support the ragged and steep edge of the Upper Grindelwald gl. Traverse R between two barriers at the highest possible level, to reach the gl. near pt. 2662m., where one can walk out on to the ice. Make a gradually rising traverse SE over the gl. The slope is easy but badly crevassed. On reaching the edge of the upper plateau, move S then SW round the lower side of the plateau, crevasses in same direction, and go into the crevassed cwm below the E side of the mtn. Go up this keeping R then L to a bergschrund under the col. Cross this and climb a steep snow/ice slope to the U. Nässijoch (4 h.). Then as for the previous rte. to summit (30 min., $4\frac{1}{2}$ h. from Gleckstein hut).

87 West-North-West Ridge (from Gwächtejoch). This ridge is a miniature Andersongrat (Schreckhorn), of comparable interest and quality on sound rock. On the N (Gleckstein) side start from the col itself, approach obvious. Coming from the S side a couloir slanting diagonally R is taken to a pt. some distance R of the col, at the foot of the steep part of the ridge. AD-, three ridge steps with pitches of III in chimneys and cracks. First ascent: C. A. Macdonald with P. & R. Almer, 17 August, 1898.

88 North/North-East Ridge. As from the foot of the cwm under E side of mtn., Rte. 86. A fine mixed climb from the Gleckstein hut, PD+, normally of the same duration as Rte. 86. Avoid the lower section over pt. 3067m. by moving on to the snow ridge from the E cwm. First ascent: J. W. S. Brady with C. & H. Kaufmann, 4 July, 1911.

NÄSSIHORN   3741m.

89 LK 1229. In the shadow of the mighty Schreckhorn, really only a prominent shoulder of the latter, but climbed often enough as a consolation prize when the big mtn. is in poor condition - this normally from the Gleckstein side.   Its SW ridge is a good technical rock climb which fast parties have been known to accomplish as a prelude to the Andersongrat. From the ridge under the Andersongrat, by a short connecting snow crest over the Nässijoch (3733m.), a few min. walk to summit.   However, by any approach, AD-.   First ascent: E. Burckhardt with C. Jossi, P. Schlegel, 2 August, 1885.

LAUTERAARSATTEL   3125m.

LK 1229, 1230.   Between the Nässihorn and Berglistock. A fine gl. pass from the Gleckstein hut to the Lauteraar hut. PD/PD+ owing to the badly crevassed condition of the gl. on both sides.   First crossing: J. Jaun, M. Bannholzer, 31 August, 1844, following first ascent of Wetterhorn.

90 From the Gleckstein hut follow Rte. 86 to the plateau of the Upper Grindelwald gl.   Cross this SE to a short wall below the pass. Either ascend this direct or more to the L where it is equally possible to cross ($4\frac{1}{2}$ h. from hut).

91 From the Lauteraar hut descend a cut path to the gl. and follow the medial moraine into the Lauteraar gl. branch. Go all the way up this in the centre to below the crevassed snow wall under the pass. Either climb direct, sometimes awkward bergschrund, on snow, ice or rocks, or trend R to an opening in the ridge above ($4\frac{1}{2}$ h. from hut).

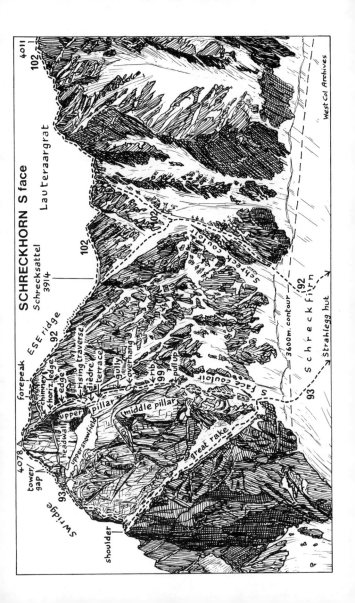

SCHRECKHORN   4078m.

LK 1229. The fabled Peak of Terror, for the average alpinist the finest rock pile in the Bernese Alps. A superb mtn. revealing a marked contrast in appearance between the mainly icy N flank and the rocky S and W flanks while both retain a handsome profile. Of their style and standard most of the climbs are hardly excelled for interest anywhere in the Alps. The rock is a red brown gneiss which is generally compact and sound. The mtn. is seldom traversed in combination with the neighbouring Lauteraarhorn but this traverse remains an outstanding expedition worthy of any party's highest ambitions. No important mtn. in the Alps has a stronger British connection. West Col Archives Memoir 2423. Rpt. Talbot, 1969.

First ascent (by a variant not used today): L. Stephen with U. Kaufmann, C. & P. Michel, 14 August, 1861. In winter: W. A. B. Coolidge with C., C. & U. Almer, F. Deutschmann, 27 January, 1879.

<u>East-South-East Ridge (Schrecksattel)</u>. A high class ordinary rte., one of the best of its style in the Alps. Superb mixed climbing with even work on snow/ice and rock. Some danger from stonefall and avalanche slope conditions in the afternoon. PD+. First ascent: C. Aeby, E. von Fellenberg, Pastor Gerwer with P. Egger, P. Inäbnit, P. Michel, 4 August, 1864 (2nd ascent of mtn.).

92 From the Strahlegg hut cross moraine and snow patches NE and enter the usually snowy and narrow Gaagg valley, on the N side of the Strahlegghorn rock ridge. Climb the snow-bed, then move L on to the easy L-hand rock ridge which is followed to the top (1½ h.). Here commences an uneven gl. band, sloping outwards above a rock barrier and overlooked by the lowest rocks of the Lauteraarhorn SW ridge. The snow-band leads N on a rising traverse to connect with the upper plateau of the Schreckfirn. In fact one has usually to negotiate the crevassed topmost part of the icefall in the gl. before the less broken plateau can be trodden. This manoeuvre may entail a short descent. Now cross the steepening plateau NE to arrive below the impressive face of ribs and couloirs 350m.

high, falling from the Schrecksattel, which is up to the L
($1\frac{1}{4}$ h.).

Above a large bergschrund, one snow tongue goes right up
into a big couloir, ill-defined in its lower part. On the R of
this is the lowest rock toe. The rocks can be climbed by any
of two or three ribs or short snow grooves between the main
couloir and the toe. The usual rte. is up the first rib R of
the couloir, but the second snow groove on the R of the second
rib (followed by its slabby rock then snow/ice crest) can be
easier. Cross the bergschrund, sometimes quite difficult, and
go up steep ice to the rib. Follow its crest, 45°, to a small
steep snowfield below a buttress, stonefall. A rising traverse
L leads into the broad upper snowbed of the main couloir, which
has a rock wall on its R. Keep close to this wall and climb
straight up to the snowy Schrecksattel (3914m.) ($1\frac{1}{2}$-2 h.).

The first part of the ridge is a series of pinnacles. From
the saddle, traverse R on steep snow or ice immediately below
the rocks, and continue thus until the ridge can be reached in
a small gap beyond this first section. This turning movement
passes along the top of the Elliotwand (J. Elliot, killed in a
fall from this pt. in 1869), which can be delicate but in favourable conditions there is a useful crevice between the ice wall
and the rocks. Half a dozen big pegs were inserted in the
rocks along this traverse in 1974. From the gap now climb
the rock ridge, sometimes icy. It is best to keep on the L
side, making short traverses, for some 100-120m., then
follow the crest, turning short steps according to preference
(II/II+). In bad conditions the entire ridge can be climbed
comfortably in crampons. Arrive at the forepeak, which is
connected to the true summit by a sharp snow ridge, 80m. long,
usually with a large cornice ($1\frac{1}{2}$ h., $5\frac{3}{4}$-$6\frac{1}{4}$ h. from Strahlegg
hut).

<u>South-West Ridge</u>. A splendid climb and a popular one for

making a simple traverse of the mtn. The ridge is in a fine position, varied and absolutely sure in good conditions. It is no longer than the ordinary rte. and clears quickly after bad weather. Rock excellent, similar to Chamonix granite. AD-, with short pitches of III. A safe descent rte. First ascent: E. H. F. Bradby, J. H. Wicks, C. Wilson, 26 July, 1902.

93 From the Strahlegg hut follow Rte. 92 to the Schreckfirn, but cross the plateau more to the W and reach the foot of a large, conspicuous snow rake/couloir, which slants up L to the ridge at a shoulder, and above its huge lower step (3 h.). Cross the bergschrund on the R, sometimes straightforward, sometimes awkward, and make a rising traverse L on snow/ice to a rockband in the couloir entrance. Normally take this R (II+) and continue up slabby rocks, often snow covered, near the R side, then work into the centre and over to the L side. Smooth slabs (II+/III) or snow (more usual) lead to a continuous snow/ice slope which is climbed to some final rocks and the ridge shoulder. In good snowy conditions, the L side of the couloir can be climbed throughout in crampons without meeting any rock pitches ($1\frac{1}{4}$ h.).

From the shoulder climb either on the crest or just L of it up the first step on magnificent rock (II) to an easier angled section. Cross this to the foot of the final step. A short narrow riser leads to a tower then a gap. In good conditions pull straight up the cracked wall in front (3m., IV), but it is normally turned L by a ledge system and a sometimes icy gully returning to the crest. The ridge is now uniformly steep and the crest gives delightful open climbing, all too brief (bits of III) to a snow ridge in two parts. Cross this delicately, cornice possible, to the summit ($1\frac{1}{2}$ h., $5\frac{3}{4}$ h. from hut).

<u>North-West Ridge (Andersongrat)</u>. A very classic rte., technically less difficult than the SW ridge but having a tedious, less sure and more serious approach. The most practised

118

rte. from the Gleckstein hut. Fine exposed climbing on the upper ridge, AD with pitches of II+/III, variable. First ascent: J.S. Anderson, G.P. Baker with U. Almer, A. Pollinger, 7 August, 1883.

94 From the Strahlegg hut descend the valley path towards the Schwarzegg ruins. Before reaching the rocks of this old site (2485m.) work to the NE and N and go into the large gl. couloir under (S of) pt. 3067m. This is the original approach to the upper Schreckfirn plateau and the normal rte. Climb this couloir which is recessed to the N of the Schreckfirn and is somewhat threatened by stonefall and falling ice. Keeping L, go through the narrows near the top (where the original ordinary rte. branched R up to the main gl.), then bear L up steep snow and rocks round the W spur of the SW ridge. This can be awkward and icy. So reach the upper Schwarzeggfirn, the hanging snowfield below the W face of the mtn. Mount this keeping somewhat R, and parallel with a bergschrund, so as to make a rising traverse to below the L side of the W face, at the same time directly below the first steep step on the NW ridge. The Nässijoch is further up to the L, above that end of the snowfield. The ridge above has been reached in numerous ways, including up the ribs further L in the vicinity of the Nässijoch. However in normal conditions it should not be necessary to opt for the latter course.

A rib with a relatively broad base comes down from near the foot of the first big ridge step. It has a narrower, subsidiary rib branch to the R, descending short of the main one. Cross the bergschrund and climb the snow slope rising between the two rib ends, then trend L on snow to cross the rocky main rib about 50m. above the top of its broad part. Continue this rising traverse L into the snow/ice couloir immediately beyond. Climb this keeping R to a narrow exit on normally snowy rocks, short, landing on the ridge below two small towers which rise into the first step. This is the normal way. In dry conditions

119

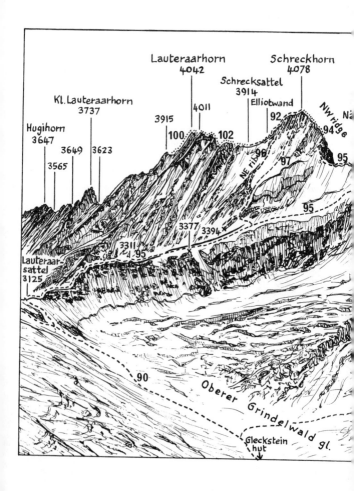

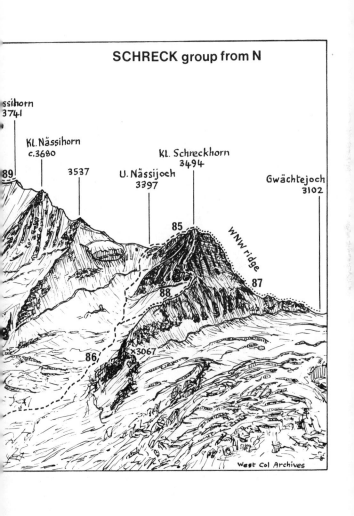

SCHRECK group from N

ssihorn
3741

Kl. Nässihorn
c.3680

89

3537

U. Nässijoch
3397

Kl. Schreckhorn
3494

Gwächtejoch
3102

85

WNW ridge

87

88

86

×3067

West Col Archives

it is more direct and quicker to climb steep snow on the immediate R of the R-hand subsidiary rib, directly into a narrow snow/rock gully. This narrows into a big steep chimney which, assumed to be free of ice, gives pitches of II+ to a pt. above the small towers and exactly at the foot of the ridge step (5 h. from Strahlegg hut).

The first step may be climbed direct by cracks and small chimneys somewhat L of crest line (III+), but it is normally turned on the L by a ledge system, a gully then reascent on icy rocks (II+). Continue over several short steps near the crest, turning difficulties on the L, till a short descent leads into a gap. Climb straight out of this by two steep pitches (III) on magnificent holds, then a few easy rocks remain before the summit snow crest is reached. Follow this delicately to the top ($2\frac{1}{2}$ h., $7\frac{1}{2}$ h. from Strahlegg hut).

95 From the Gleckstein hut follow Rtes. 86, 90 to the Lauteraarsattel ($4\frac{1}{2}$ h.). Now go up the mixed snow/rock ridge running SW to pt. 3311m., where it becomes broad and all snow. Continue keeping L of the edge to a bergschrund below the Nässihorn. Climb a fairly steep snow/ice slope to the Nässijoch depression immediately L of the Nässihorn. Continue along a fine sharp ridge in little steps which turns to rock when two small towers are reached where the Strahlegg hut approach arrives. Climb the towers direct (II+) to the foot of the first steep step where Rte. 94 is joined. Or, more usual, turn the towers on the L side and go straight into the ledge system which avoids the first ridge step ($2\frac{1}{2}$ h., 7 h. from Gleckstein hut). Continue as for Rte. 94 ($2\frac{1}{2}$ h., $9\frac{1}{2}$ h. from Gleckstein hut).

North-East Rib. The original rte. on this side of the mtn. It has never become popular and appears to be rarely climbed. More direct but less sure than the Andersongrat. Good snow and snow free rocks are necessary for a comfortable ascent. AD/AD+, exposed, average angle 48°. First ascent: R. & W. M. Pendlebury with P. Baumann, P. Kaufmann, 11 July, 1873. Descended by C. A. Macdonald with C. Jossi, J. Taugwalder, 25 July, 1890.

96 From the Gleckstein hut follow Rtes. 86, 90, 95 to the Lauteraarsattel and along the ridge towards the Nässihorn until one can walk L on snow. Turn off Rte. 95 at c. 3450m. and traverse easy snow S, under the ice cliffs of the NE face, to a rock rib extending down still further below the height of the traverse undertaken (6 h.). Climb easily on to this rib at c. 3500m. and go up it pleasantly with alternate snow/ice bits to the level of the ice cliffs further R. Trend L off the rib across a steep shallow snow/ice gully and reach rocks of the next rib L. Climb these with snow/ice bits till the rocks peter out and another snow/ice gully must be crossed L to reach the main rib on the face. This is narrow and quite distinct. Follow it with pitches of II on good rock to a temporary fading in snow/ice again. Climb direct to the rocks of the rib emerging again, now generally icy and follow these along the crest line in an exposed situation to the ESE ridge which is reached at the forepeak (Rte. 92) (3-4½ h., 9-10 h. from Gleckstein hut).

North-East Face. A fine ice climb, rarely done only because of its remoteness; 5½-6 h. from Gleckstein hut, not much less from Lauteraar hut. 550m., D+, average angle 53°. First ascent: I. & J. Taguchi with S. Brawand, C. Kaufmann, 26 August, 1938 (6 h.). In winter: K. Güngerich and three others, 8 March, 1974 (10 h. from biv. at foot of face, descending same rte. latterly in darkness by abseils, in 5 h.). First British ascent: R. Milward, S. Parr, July, 1977.

97 Reach the foot of the face as for Rte. 96 and follow Rte. 96 to where it moves L off the first rib across a shallow ice gully.

Continue ascending direct, past the upper edge of the ice cliffs, to the L end of a bergschrund which slants up R across the face. Cross the schrund and make a rising traverse R above it, going steeply into the middle of the face. Reach some small rock outcrops in the middle part, turn these on the R and go up their R side on fluted ice with rock bits towards a continuous rib coming down furthest in the summit line. If conditions permit it is better to steepen the lower rising traverse R and pass above these outcrops and minor ribs. Either way, now aim for the rib to L of summit line one, then go into the ice gully between them. Original finish: trend R and climb the L side of the main R-hand rib, on icy rock to reach the top about 3 min. L of the summit. Subsequent parties have found a more pleasant finish by following, from the entrance to the dividing ice gully, a shallow gully just L of the L-hand rib, finishing 5 min. L of the summit (6-7 h. from foot of face).

98 <u>West Face</u>. This flank is cut centrally in its lower half by a large ice gully with a dividing rock rib separating two branches which higher up both bend L and almost rejoin under the NW ridge. This line to the ridge was climbed by O. Hug, W. Weckert; W. Rickenbach, A. Simmen, 8 July, 1935. D, with pitches of IV/IV+. A direct line to the summit, from where the gully bends L, was climbed by E. Hupf with H. Schlunegger, 25 September, 1941. D+ with pitches of V. Other variations have been made on the face, which is exposed to stonefall and not recommended.

<u>South Face Pillar Direct</u>. The original rte. on the S face trends L up the fine steep slabby wall of the middle pillar to reach the prominent snowfield under the headwall to L of upper pillar. From near the upper L end of this snowfield it ascends the headwall, first to a snowband fairly low down, by a

prominent dièdre in its L side, finishing at the first snow crest at the top of the SW ridge. A good rte. on excellent rock, a bit complicated, stonefall negligible. D, with pitches of IV+. K. Blach, K. Reiss, 17 July, 1950 (6 h.). The obvious couloir flanking the R side of the S face pillar is a serious mixed climb, D+, probably unrepeated. E. & W. Reiss, A. Reist, H. Sollberger, 27 July, 1949 (6 h.).

The direct rte. is finer than either of the foregoing and is rated by the Swiss as the best rock climb of its standard on a high mtn. in the Bernese Alps. Mostly excellent gneiss, dries quickly after bad weather, stonefall negligible. D/D+ with pitches of IV, one of V and moves of V. First ascent: W. Munter, E. & D. Schmied, 17 July, 1964 (6½ h.). Has been climbed at least 20 times.

99 Start exactly as for Rte. 93, where the bergschrund is crossed at R side to move up L on snow/ice to reach the rock-band under the couloir leading to the SW ridge shoulder (3 h. from Strahlegg hut). Go straight above the bergschrund to cross the foot of the narrow opening to the S face couloir, moving L over snow/rock to reach the flattish rib bordering L side of couloir. Climb this rib pleasantly with bits on steep snow to the foot of the R hand edge of the middle pillar (there is no lower section), immediately adjoining the couloir.

Work up R, round the steep pillar base with an overhanging pull up (II), to reach steep snow at L side of couloir. Climb this for two rope lengths keeping L, to a subsidiary slabby rib projecting into couloir. Take the rib for 3 short pitches, to where it steepens. Traverse R along a small ledge to a parallel rib. Climb this for a few m. into a groove below an overhang, then trend L below overhang into a gully. Follow gully for 2 pitches (III, IV) to a terrace (snow) below a steep step. Move L for 20m. then climb a few m. to a steep dièdre. Climb this for 30m. (V, 4 pegs, crux) into a recess below a roof. Make a rising traverse R across a small vertical wall

(V, peg), and continue rising steeply R over smooth rock to
the R edge of the upper pillar. Climb the edge by a smooth
slab with thin cracks (5m., V, 2 pegs) and continue direct for
2 pitches (III) to a horizontal ledge marking end of the snowy
ledge system running L across the upper pillar headwall. The
sharp smooth ridge above is turned on the R by taking a vertical chimney (IV), leading back to the crest. A technically
easier but loose and unprotected variation can be made by
moving diagonally L from foot of chimney up grey slabs to
reach the crest. Continue on the crest up a steep step (IV)
followed by a short descent into a gap. From here by easy
rocks in the same line to the snow crest at the top of the SW
ridge (6-7 h. from bergschrund, 9-10 h. from Strahlegg hut).

LAUTERAARHORN   4042m.

LK 1229, 1249.   This peak is like a Siamese-twin to the
Schreckhorn, and there are some physical similarities. They
are joined by a long and high pinnacled ridge and there is a
tolerable degree of symmetry about the pair when seen from
at least two directions. In fact there is hardly anything to
compare between climbing on the two peaks. The rock of the
Lauteraarhorn is often poor but some of it is good. The mtn.
is awkward of access and all rtes. are fairly long. It is climbed
much less frequently than the Schreckhorn, and more ascents
are probably made from the Lauteraar hut side.
    First ascent: E. Desor, M. Girard, A. Escher von der
Linth with M. Bannholzer, D. Brigger, Fahner, J. Leuthold,
J. Madutz, 8 August, 1842. Not repeated until 1869. In winter:
Mrs. E.P. Jackson, E. Boss with U. Almer, J. Kaufmann,
5 January, 1888. On ski: F. Thormann, 1925.

<u>South Couloir and South-East Ridge</u>. The easiest rte. but re-
mote from large huts and most convenient from the new Aar
biv. hut. An interesting enough expedition, worthwhile, PD.
The S flank needs a good covering of firm snow, otherwise
loose shaly rock is exposed, rendering the ascent one of the
most tedious ordinary rtes. in the Bernese Alps. The

Strahleggpass rte. supplies both approaches. First ascension-ists.

100 From the Strahlegg hut follow Rte. 103 to the Strahleggpass and descend to the Strahlegg gl., Rte. 104. From the foot of the Strahleggpass rock wall contour the gl. to the E and soon reach a prominent triangle of snow rising into the S flank of the mtn. ($3\frac{1}{4}$ h.). Climb to the top of the triangle, cross a bergschrund and continue up a rock couloir, stonefall possible, often snowy, trending R up to a broad snow rib. Still trending R, this leads into the large open S couloir at mid-height. Climb the steep snow couloir and rocks to a small snow saddle on the SE ridge immediately L of pt. 3915m., near the foot of the last riser to the summit ($2\frac{3}{4}$ h.). Follow the crest via a gap and a nice slab pitch to top (1 h., 7 h. from Strahlegg hut).

From the Aar biv. hut follow Rte. 104 as for the Strahleggpass, to the foot of the S couloir at c. 3060m., not far from the rock wall below the col ($2\frac{1}{2}$ h.). Climb the couloir or a rock rib on its L, up through the narrows and into the broad middle section, where the Strahlegg hut approach joins the couloir from the broad snow rib on the L (hut to summit, 6 h.).

<u>South-West Ridge.</u> A somewhat artificial rock climb, in that it can be left at the foot of its almost vertical upper steps by an interesting traverse across the S face to the SE ridge. This variation is recommended and is the shortest rte. of reasonable standard from the Strahlegg hut. AD. The direct finish is D, with pitches of IV/IV+. Ridge direct: E. F. L. Fankhauser with C. Jossi, 5 October, 1900.

101 From the Strahlegg hut follow Rte. 103 to the Strahleggpass (2 h.). Climb on to the easy angled ridge which is followed with pitches of II on quite good rock, and some snow crests, to a scree shoulder at the foot of the first of two big steps rising to the summit ($1\frac{1}{2}$ h.). Now traverse R on to the S face, descending at first in a steep snow and rock couloir, round a rib, then horizontally along a snowy slab line under a series of buttresses and ribs, also crossing a couloir to reach another couloir at a corner below the SE ridge. All this section is variable according to conditions, normally delicate. Climb this last couloir or a rib on its L to the ridge which is reached not far above the saddle beside pt. 3915m. The ridge leads in 45 min. to summit (2-2½ h., 5½-6 h. from Strahlegg hut). A good descent rte.

Direct: At the foot of the first step, move L of the crest on to a wall and climb a difficult chimney/crack. Rejoin the ridge which is followed to the upper shoulder at the foot of the final step. Traverse 10m. L on to the side wall, then climb straight up for 10m., difficult, then trend L to a short crack. Climb this with difficulty, then another crack to the R which leads on to the crest at a shelf. This shelf goes out across the W wall for some distance. Climb straight up a difficult and delicate couloir, leading to the summit (3 h., 6½ h. from Strahlegg hut).

North-West Ridge (Lauteraargrat). The classic rte. up the mtn. In good conditions a fast party can climb the Schreckhorn by its SW ridge, continue to the Lauteraarhorn, and descend to the Strahlegg hut in a day. Normally a good deal shorter by starting in the ordinary way from the Schrecksattel. The ridge consists of several large towers and pinnacles and many smaller ones, about 50 in all. The rock is mainly good on the crest, with some brittle sections, but is uniformly shattered and rotten on the flanks. A more or less direct traverse on the crest over all the gendarmes is recommended. AD, with pitches of III and moves of III+.

First ascent, two parties moving in opposite directions on the same day: (N-S) Frln. H. Kuntze with P. & R. Bernet; (S-N) Miss G. L. Bell with H. & U. Fuhrer, 24 July, 1902.

"Frln. Kuntze went to Grindelwald ... having telegraphed for guides, and my two are persuaded that she is bent on the same expedition from the other side. I shall laugh if we meet half way across the arête, but I shall not be at all surprised" (from Letters of Gertrude Bell). A commentator noted later that "the meeting on the ridge was not greeted with enthusiasm".

102 From the Strahlegg hut follow Rte. 92 to the Schrecksattel. In good conditions it is more usual to climb a broad snow groove, becoming a couloir, to reach the ridge in a tiny gap, close to the first step. This direct variation starts from the pt. where a rising traverse L is made on the normal rte. to reach the upper snow couloir of the Schrecksattel. Instead, trend R up a snow and rock rib into the groove slope which leads as indicated to the ridge (50°, AD) ($4\frac{3}{4}$ h.). If reaching the ridge at the usual saddle, the first section of the crest is fairly easy, over half a dozen small towers, along to the pt. where the variation arrives.

Climb the first main ridge step direct, over mini towers and continue along a serrated crest to the top of the first section (4011m.). Descend by the crest to a gap at the foot of a large square tower (4015m., LK 50). Turn its slabby wall on the L and on this side climb a few m. to a tiny ledge. From here surmount a short overhang and pull up to the top of the slabby wall. Continue directly above in a smooth chimney to the top of the tower. Descend with an awkward slab (abseil) to a gap and reach the top of the next tower by climbing on the R (W) flank. Continue on the crest over three towers, then descend steeply to a deep gap (3988m.) and climb a small tower on its R side. A number of small gaps and tower/steps follow with no special difficulty, all taken along the crest. Descend to a final depression in front of the summit pile and go directly up the latter to top (average $4\frac{1}{2}$ h. from Schreck-sattel, $9\frac{1}{4}$ h. from Strahlegg hut).

STRAHLEGGPASS 3340m.

LK 1229, 1249. The pass lies at the foot of the SW ridge of the Lauteraarhorn with the Strahlegghorn just beyond. The classic rte. from Grindelwald to the Grimsel via the Strahlegg and Lauteraar huts. It is easier than the Finsteraarjoch. Both sides, F, except that the rock wall on the E side requires care, PD. First tourist crossing: R. Meyer with A. Abbühl, K. Huber, 3 September, 1812.

103 From the Strahlegg hut cross moraine and snow patches NE and enter the usually snowy and narrow Gaagg valley, on the N side of the Strahlegghorn rock ridge. Climb the snow-bed, then move L on to the easy L-hand rock ridge which is followed to the top ($1\frac{1}{2}$ h.). Now climb a snow slope to the R (E) and reach the obvious pass (30 min., 2 h. from Strahlegg hut).

104 From the Aar biv. hut descend to the Strahlegg gl. and follow its R side without incident to snow slopes under the S flank of the Lauteraarhorn. Climb to the foot of the snowy couloir/rock wall below the pass in the top L-hand corner ($3\frac{1}{4}$ h.). This wall is 150m. high and about $50°$ steep. Cross the bergschrund and, according to conditions, climb either the couloir on the L (when there is a lot of snow on the rocks), or the rocks by ribs and small gullies somewhat to the R, almost anywhere; steep, a bit loose, traces of path (45 min., 4 h. from Aar biv. hut, $5\frac{1}{2}$ h. from Lauteraar hut).

STRAHLEGGHORN 3461.2m.

105 LK 1229. One of the finest viewpoints of easy access in the Grindelwald district. A very popular excursion. From the Strahleggpass, Rtes. 103, 104, by the steep and narrow N ridge, mainly loose rock with pitches of II and snow/ice bits, in 1 h. (PD). More easily from the Strahlegg hut direct, by climbing straight up the snowy S flank, then moving L on to the SW ridge at an obvious snowy pt., then up this short ridge to top, F+. All ways from Strahlegg hut to summit take $3-3\frac{1}{2}$ h.

130

F. O. Schuster with P. Baumann, C. Bernet (followed by another party), 14 August, 1888, found a bottle on the summit containing the card of a Swiss climber who made the ascent in September, 1887 - the bottle was accidentally knocked down and lost before the name could be recorded.

KLEIN LAUTERAARHORN   3737m.

106 LK 1229.   This mtn. has in fact sharp multiple summits not marked on map, between ridge pts. 3649 and 3623. In this direction formerly measured as twins, 3734m. and 3728m., then a sharp shoulder 3714m., finally pt. 3737m. above the gap 3623m. Seldom climbed, easiest rte. AD. Several interesting mixed rtes. of D grade. First ascent: P. Montandon, A. Weber, R. von Wyss, 2 July, 1904. The last high summit of the Bernese Alps to be climbed.

HUGIHORN   3647m.

107 LK 1229.   Marked but not named on map. A fairly significant ridge summit with an obvious ordinary rte. up the Hugi gl. (not named on map), which forms the S side of the mtn., coming down near the Aar biv. hut. By this gl. and finishing up the SW ridge, or directly up the rocky headwall of the gl., or L on to S ridge. PD. First ascent, P. Montandon & party, 1897.

LAUTERAAR-ROTHÖRNER   3473m.   3466.6m.

LK 1249, 1250.   Terminal ridge pts. of the Lauteraarhörner, directly above the Aar biv. hut. First ascent: P. Montandon, A. Weber, R. von Wyss, 1 July, 1904.

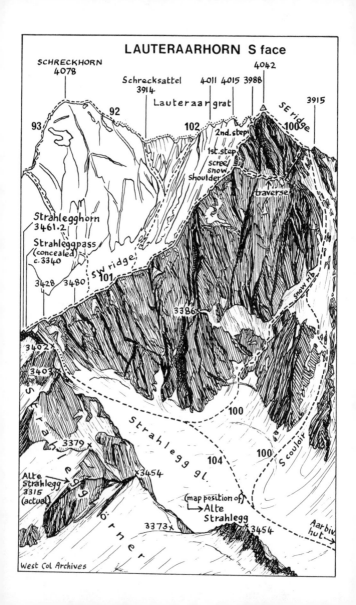

LAUTERAARHORN S face

SCHRECKHORN
4078

Schrecksattel
3914

4011 4015 3988

4042

Lauteraar grat

SE ridge

3915

93   92   102   100e

2nd. step

1st. step

scree
snow
shoulder

traverse

Strahlegghorn
3461.2

Strahleggpass
(concealed
c.3340)

SW ridge

101

3428 3480

snow rib

3386

3402 x

3403 x

S couloir

100

3379 x

Strahlegg gl.

104

100

x3454

Alte
Strahlegg
3315 (actual)

Strahlegghörner

(map position of)
Alte
Strahlegg

3373 x

x3454

Aar biv
hut

West Col Archives

Wetterhörner

The collective name originally for three peaks and now extended to five, of which the Mittelhorn is highest but of which the Wetterhorn is the best known and grandest in appearance - allowing for the contribution made by the bastions of the Scheideggwetterhorn. The Berglistock is somewhat detached from the others but offers its main climbing interest to the group focal pt. of the Gleckstein hut. Most of the climbs on these peaks are made from the Grindelwald side but the Dossen hut (Rosenlaui) and Gauli hut (Haslital) are useful alternative starting pts.

SCHEIDEGGWETTERHORN   3361m.

LK 1229. Once nicknamed the "Grindelwald Dru", its present name being given by Coolidge. An immense shoulder of the Wetterhorn presenting an impressive triangular limestone wall about 1300m. high above the Gr. Scheidegg pass between Grindelwald and Rosenlaui. The most conspicuous sight from the Grindelwald valley, not excepting the Eiger. The original rte. is from the rear, i.e. S, but all rtes. are difficult and of a character not in keeping with the rest of the Wetterhörner. Regarded in mountaineering as an independent summit. A number of the big rock rtes. on the NW wall are described in the "Engelhörner" guide (1968). The original rte. from the Gleckstein hut is described below. First ascent: G. A. Hasler with P. Bernet, C. Jossi, 13 May, 1901. The second ascent was not made until 1929, being the occasion when the NW face was climbed for the first time.

<u>Original Route</u>. Rarely climbed but the mandatory descent for parties completing a rte. on the NW face. Hasler climbed the wall to the ridge somewhat L of the access gully, using an artificial aid consisting of a thick stake with nails driven into it. His party took 13 h. from Gleckstein hut to summit. The rock is either terribly smooth or incredibly bad. In ascent, as described, AD+ with short moves of IV+ using pegs. In

descent, AD with abseils. Stonefall in the couloir, and a party coming down has to be very careful about dislodging rock on to itself.

108 From the Gleckstein hut a small but good track climbs grass then stony slopes NE and duly arrives among slabby barriers below the Krinnen (Chrinnen) gl. Plenty of cairns mark the way on to the gl., somewhat L of pt. 2663m. (LK 50) ($1\frac{1}{4}$ h.). Ascend L below the edge of the gl. and only mount it on approaching the ridge which bounds the N side of the gl. slope to below the enclosing ridge where a gully comes down between two steps on the ridge above, lower down than pt. 3053m. Climb a pitch L of the gully, then move up R to reach the ridge on the upper step. Follow the crest easily to pt. 3053m. and into a little gap beyond ($1\frac{1}{2}$ h.). On the other side descend briefly to the Hühnergutz (Gutz) gl. and cross this NE, normally icy and crevassed, and with a fresh snow covering very delicate, to the rock wall at the back. This wall is cut by a gully rising to a prominent gap (c. 3370m.) in the ridge above between pt. 3455m. and the summit further L. The wall is about 150m. high. In descent it is best to use the gully, abseiling where necessary. In ascent it is preferable to climb the rock wall just L of it. You can get halfway up without too much difficulty, depending on snow conditions, but the last 50m. is very smooth rock. Climb this section with peg belays and peg handholds, trending R to finish at the ridge gap (2-3 h.). Now follow the crest, very loose, to a gap then a thin toppling gendarme. Traverse this delicately and descend to a gap before another similar pinnacle/step. Traverse this on terrible rock to a comfortable descending crest which is followed briefly to the summit (1 h., $5\frac{3}{4}$-$6\frac{3}{4}$ h. from hut. In descent, about 5 h.).

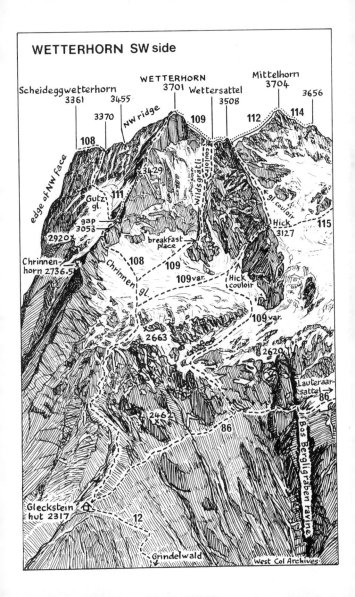

WETTERHORN SW side

Scheideggwetterhorn
3361

3370

3455

WETTERHORN
3701

Wettersattel
3508

Mittelhorn
3704

3656

NW ridge

108

109

112

114

edge of NW face

3429

Wildsgrätli

gl couloir

111

couloir

Gutz.
gl.

gap
3053

2920 X

breakfast
place

Hick
3127

115

Chrinnen-
horn 2736.5

Chrinnen

108

109

Hick
couloir

gl.

109 var.

109 var.

X
2663

109 var.

X
2620

Lauteraar-
sattel
86

X
2462

86

Gleckstein
hut 2317

12

Grindelwald

Bas Bergligräben ravine

West Col Archives

WETTERHORN 3701m.

LK 1229. The fabled Peak of Tempests. It still seems that the correct name for this peak is the Hasli Jungfrau, but common usage and its pre-eminent position above the Grindelwald valley have led to the adoption of a singular version of the collective name Wetterhörner. Though not quite the highest summit of the group, the Wetterhorn is monumental in appearance and more conspicuous than its neighbours. It is also climbed much more frequently. An essential peak for Grindelwald parties, mixed climbing, none of it altogether easy, and most of the rock, when it has to be used, is very rotten. A superb viewpoint. West Col Archives Memoir 922.

First ascent: M. Bannholzer, J. Jaun, 31 August, 1844 (up Rosenlaui gl.). In winter: Miss M. C. Brevoort, W. A. B. Coolidge with C. Almer father & son and 3 porters, 15 January, 1874. On ski: H. Hoek, C. Schiller with J. Moor, A. Tännler, 26 January, 1903. The early climbing history is full of disputes and counterclaims by Alpine historians. The famous ascent by Alfred Wills in 1854 was probably the 3rd, and almost certainly the first from Grindelwald. Some evidence suggests two earlier ascents from Grindelwald, one by the Englishman E. J. Blackwell. At all events, prior to these was the Agassiz party ascent, the true 2nd, from Grimsel across the Lauteraarsattel in 1845. Winston Churchill with C. Kaufmann climbed the mtn. in 1894.

<u>South-South-East Ridge (Wettersattel)</u>. The usual rte. from either the Gleckstein or Dossen huts. It can be reached by a much longer approach from the Gauli hut. Several variations are used to reach the Wettersattel (3508m.), according to conditions, on the Gleckstein side. A very popular climb, some stonefall danger on latter approach. PD. First complete ascent from Grindelwald: A. Wills with A. Balmat, P. Bohren, U. Lauener, A. Simond, joined by C. Almer, U. Kaufmann, carrying the subsequently famous fir tree, 17 September, 1854. An important date and meeting in Alpine climbing history. The first ascensionists made the Rosenlaui gl. approach.

109 From the Gleckstein hut a good but small track climbs grass then stony slopes NE and duly arrives among the slabby barriers below the Krinnen (Chrinnen) gl. Plenty of cairns mark the way on to the gl., somewhat L of pt. 2663m. (LK 50)

$(1\frac{1}{4}$ h.). Cross the easy gl. to the L (NW) side of a broken rock spur called Wildsgrätli, jutting from the face into the gl. On the R of this is the Wetterhorn couloir, and further R is the large spur containing the gap called Hick, which marks the R-hand side of the face. In a corner below the face climb R on steep rocks, a bit loose, and reach the crest of the Wildsgrätli above its foot. Traditional breakfast place. Climb the spur for 75m. then trend R, rising along a break in the steepness of the rocks forming the L side of the Wetterhorn couloir. Higher up, cross the couloir, stonefall possible and sometimes awkward, and climb a rib of broken rocks on the R side directly to the Wettersattel at the top $(2\frac{1}{2}$ h., $3\frac{3}{4}$ h. from Gleckstein hut).

In good conditions it is quicker and safer, but steeper, to continue straight up the Wildsgrätli spur to below the rock wall under the SSE ridge. Some good hard snow may be found on the broad slope of the spur. Near the top, trend R on steep rocks and snow, and finally go up a short snow couloir forming a vague weakness at the R-hand end of the rock wall, on to the SSE ridge at a point just above the Wettersattel, PD/PD+. More direct exits can be made on to the ridge higher up, pitches of III/III+.

Early in the season, when there is a lot of snow on either of the two approaches described above, the usual rte. is by the Hick couloir. One can either reach the Krinnen gl. by the usual way, or go along the approach to the Lauteraarsattel, Rte. 86, to within a short distance of the Bos Bergligraben ravine; then climb to the S end of the Krinnen gl., somewhat L of pt. 2620m. Either way, reach the couloir which descends from the gap called Hick (3127m.) in the ridge bordering the R-hand side of the mtn. Climb the 200m. snow couloir to the gap, stonefall when clear of snow. Now cross snow and climb the big gl. couloir rising to the N, with the Hick spur on its L. This slope is steep at the top and finishes near the

Wettersattel. In the right conditions this is the easiest of all the approaches, and may also be the quickest means of descent. With little snow it can be quite unpleasant and is an accident spot for unwary parties.

From the Wettersattel climb the broad snow ridge which soon narrows and steepens. It is often icy. Turn a group of rocks on the R, but a direct ascent is often possible, and re-ascend to the L. Now climb direct, then move a little R on some rocks, often snow covered, and finally direct again. The last slope is short and very steep and is crowned by a cornice. Do not stand on highest pt. if the cornice is large (45 min., $4\frac{1}{2}$-5 h. from Gleckstein hut).

110 Starting from the Dossen hut, follow a track under S side of ridge then go up snow and rocks below ridge, skirting projections to the L, to reach the Dossensattel immediately below pt. 3032m. ($1\frac{1}{4}$ h.). On the W side go down a steep snow/ice couloir, sometimes scree at end of season, for 100m. to the Rosenlaui gl. plateau (30 min.). Cross the gl. bowl, called the Wetterkessel, to the SW, crevassed, and reach by a steep snow slope the Wellhornsattel (c. 3220m.), which is above the end of the last (S) rocks of the Wellhorn (1 h.). Now cross gl. slopes to the W and climb SW through a narrow snow cwm leading to the Wettersattel at its head ($1\frac{1}{2}$ h., $4\frac{1}{4}$ h. from Dossen hut). Now follow the previous rte. up the ridge (45 min., 5 h. from hut).

111 West-South-West Ridge. A rte. climbed from time to time in the past, and in the past has had two fixed ropes placed on it to encourage more ascents. These ropes are now probably missing. Above pt. 3053m. it forms an initial step, followed by three tower steps up to a final regular ridge. The second tower is pt. 3429m. The climbing is mostly on very bad rock and the key pitch is sensationally exposed. D/D+ with pitches of IV and bits of V. The initial step, rarely climbed, is V.

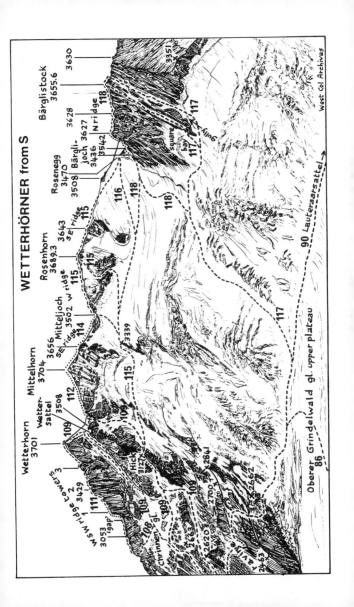

WETTERHÖRNER from S

Wetterhorn 3701
WSW ridge towers 3 2 1 3429
3053
gap
Chrinnen gl.
2263
2620
2700
2700
2841
2552
2463

Wetter-sattel 3508

Mittelhorn 3704

Mitteljoch SE ridge 3502 W ridge
3656

Rosenhorn 3689.3

Rosenegg 3470
3508

Bärgli-joch 3436 3542

Bärglistock 3655.6

3630
3351
3628
3627

N ridge

square bay

gully

109
112
111
109
109
108
109
109
Hick 3127

115
3339

114
115

115
115

116
118

118

117
117

117

117

118

90 Lauteraarsattel

86
Oberer Grindelwald gl. upper plateau

West Col Archives

First ascent: S. Uramatsu with S. Brawand, E. Steuri, 24 August, 1928 (9 h. from Gleckstein hut).

Approach by Rte. 108 to the first snow bay L of the ridge and above the Hühnergutz gl. (3¼ h.). From the top of this bay go up tricky slabs, short steps (ice) and rubble bearing R to a dièdre slanting L. Climb this (IV) to reach the crest above the initial step and between the 1st and 2nd towers. Go up the 2nd tower somewhat on the L side (II+) to the gap behind it. Cross this gap, awkward dislocation, icy, and continue up a mixed ridge of moderate steepness to the foot of the 3rd tower. The R side of this is cut by a steep crack about 70m. long (not round the snowy ledgeband further R). Climb the crack with pitches of IV and short bits of V to the top of the tower. Descend a short snow/ice crest to a saddle, followed by a fine mixed crest to the summit.

MITTELHORN 3704m.

LK 1229. The highest peak of the Wetterhörner, climbed quite often, sometimes in combination with the Wetterhorn, which adds very little to the overall time spent on the latter mtn. First ascent: S. T. Speer with K. Abplanalp, J. Jaun, J. Michel, 8 or 9 July, 1845. Overshadowed by the Wetterhorn affair, an ascent greatly underestimated in the annals of mountaineering. In winter on ski: Bergans, Risler, 18 December, 1912.

West Flank. The shortest rte. from the Gleckstein hut and the usual way from the Dossen hut. PD to the Wettersattel, then F. First ascensionists.

112 From the Gleckstein or Dossen huts reach the Wettersattel by Rtes. 109 or 110 (3¾ h. or 4¼ h.). Climb snow slopes to a rock ridge with snow, leading pleasantly to summit (45 min. from Wettersattel).

113 North-East Ridge. From the Dossen hut it is shorter and no more difficult to climb the NE ridge. By Rte. 110 the Well-hornsattel is approached but not crossed. Move into the gl. bay under (S of) the ridge which is reached above its lower step, pt. 3369m., and followed by the crest to summit ($4\frac{3}{4}$ h. from Dossen hut).

114 <u>South-East Ridge</u>. Runs down to the Mitteljoch (3502m.). An uneven rock climb, mainly PD but with a big rock step up to pt. 3656m. Taken direct, this is IV/IV+ but it can be turned by an awkward traverse movement on either flank, III+, short. Normally this ridge is descended, abseils convenient and easy, in the course of making the Wetterhörner traverse ($1\frac{1}{2}$-2 h. up or down from Mitteljoch).

ROSENHORN   3689.3m.

LK 1229. Probably the least frequented peak of the Wetter-hörner, normally crossed when doing the classic Wetterhörner triple summit traverse. First ascent: E. Desor, D. Dollfus-Ausset, Dupasquier, Stengel with M. Bannholzer, J. Jaun, J. Währen and 3 other guides, 28 August, 1844. On ski: C. Erb, G. Leuch, R. Wyss, 24 April, 1908.

115 The shortest rte. from the Gleckstein hut is directly up the SW flank to summit, pleasant rock and snow, PD. Access via Hick couloir, Rte. 109 then a rising traverse over the gl. below the Mittelhorn, going over two terrace/steps, the first taken just above the level of Hick, the second above pt. 3339m.

From this approach the Mitteljoch (3502m.) can also be reached, and the W ridge followed with a pleasant scramble giving pitches of III in $1\frac{1}{2}$ h. to summit. From the Dossen hut the Mitteljoch is easily reached over the Rosenlaui gl. from Rte. 110.

The first ascensionists' and easiest rte. is up the SE ridge from the Rosenegg saddle (3470m.), F/F+. By this ridge, about $5\frac{1}{2}$ h. from either hut.

ROSENEGG 3470m.

116 LK 1229. A saddle at the SE foot of the Rosenhorn and before the first uplift of the Berglistock N ridge which starts at the Berglijoch (3436m.). From the Hick couloir of Rte. 109, access by the high level gl. traverse indicated in Rte. 115, $4\frac{1}{2}$ h. from Gleckstein hut. First crossing: F. Jacomb with C. Michel, J. Zwalt, 4 August, 1863.

Wetterhörner Traverse

A classic expedition from the Gleckstein hut, of no great difficulty, over the Wetterhorn, Mittelhorn and Rosenhorn. It is normally done in the W-E direction, as this simplifies the Mittelhorn SE ridge section which is then taken in descent (Rte. 114, above), finishing at the Rosenegg saddle from where one descends as indicated in Rte. 116. The Mittelhorn SE ridge can be avoided by a detour to the Wellhornsattel and re-ascent to the Mitteljoch, which is done in most cases. Round trip from Gleckstein and back, 12 h. in good snow conditions. First traverse: S. Spencer with C. Jossi, U. Kaufmann, 22 July, 1894.

BERGLISTOCK 3655.6m.

LK 1229, 1230. Bärglistock. An elongated rock ridge, more imposing than either the Mittelhorn or Rosenhorn. The ridge has several secondary and not much lower summits than the highest pt. Climbed quite frequently. Fair to good rock, gneiss. First ascent: C. Aeby with P. Egger, P. Inäbnit, 26 September, 1864. British party, 3rd ascent: F. Pollock with P. Baumann, P. Rubi, 26 August, 1868. On ski: A. Lunn with P. Bernet, 24 April, 1922.

West Face. The ordinary and easiest rte. from the Gleckstein hut, a pleasant and popular climb. PD. First ascensionists.

117 From the Gleckstein hut follow Rte. 86 as for the Lauteraarsattel, and cross the Upper Grindelwald gl. more to the E, large crevasses in same direction. Turn a large group of crevasses L by going straight up in the direction of the Rosenegg saddle, then return R (S) and go slightly downward to below a narrow band of ice cliffs along the foot of a square-cut gl. bay in the W face (4 h.).

Further R, beyond the rock toe marking R side of the gl. bay, a long open gully cuts the W face R (S) of the summit line. Cross a bergschrund and climb the L side of this gully, stonefall. Keep to rocks on the L side where possible and reach the ridge gap at the top. Follow ridge for a few min. to summit ($1\frac{1}{2}$ h., $5\frac{1}{2}$ h. from Gleckstein hut).

It is sometimes better but more difficult to climb the rock rib on the L (N) side of the gully, direct to the summit. The rib is not entirely continuous and the mixed ground connections can be tricky. Reach the rib from the L, by first entering the gl. bay beyond its ice cliffs, then move up R over easy rock to its crest. Generally PD with short pitches of III (2 h. up rib to summit).

North Ridge (from Berglijoch). An interesting and pleasant rock scramble, useful for making a traverse of the mtn. and the most direct way from the Dossen hut. PD+ with short pitches of III. Easier in descent. First ascent: W. W. Graham with P. Baumann father & son, 30 September, 1886.

118 From the Gleckstein hut follow Rte. 117 to just below the SW side of the Rosenegg saddle. Alternatively, it can be quicker to start by Rte. 109 and take the Hick couloir variation for the high level gl. traverse mentioned in Rte. 115 (about 4 h.).

From the Dossen hut follow Rte. 110 as for the Wetterhorn

but go up the L side of the Rosenlaui gl., under the Dossen, to the adjoining Renfenjoch (3052m.). When the gl. is in poor condition a recommended alternative is to traverse the ridge of the Dossen, from the Dossensattel to the Renfenjoch. Continue up the long gl. slopes SW, passing close to the West Wetterlimmi, and so reach the Rosenegg saddle (3470m.). Cross to the other side and join the Gleckstein approach (about 5 h.).

Now contour gl. slopes S/SW to below the W side of   the Berglijoch, then climb to this gap by a short chimney/crack in 20 min. The ridge is long and rises in numerous short steps. If the crest is followed precisely there are pitches of IV; these are normally turned either L or R, never far from crest. There are several delicate snow/ice saddles, all sure. Follow the ridge without particular incident and on good rock, over pt. 3628m., to the summit (2½ h. from Berglijoch, 1½ h. in descent. From Gleckstein hut, 7 h.   From Dossen hut, 8 h.).

WETTERLIMMI   3250m.

119 LK 1229, 1230.   A sloping snow saddle formed by the Rosenlaui and Gauli gls., between the Rosenegg saddle and the Renfenhorn. The correct passage is the West saddle, immediately SW of rock pt. 3250m. The original passage lies in a narrow snow neck now with a headwall immediately NE of this pt. It is the easiest passage from the Rosenlaui gl. and Dossen hut to the Gauli gl. and hut. In the context of the guidebook the approach on the Gauli hut side would be used in starting from that hut to reach any of the Wetterhörner peaks and the Berglistock. From the saddle the connections to these peaks are on easy but crevassed slopes and are obvious from map.

At all times use the SW saddle. Gauli hut to Wetterlimmi, about 4½ h., F+. The rte. is easy and follows the long crevassed slopes of the Gauli gl. From Dossen hut to saddle, as for Rte. 118 to the Berglistock, with a slight deviation, F+/PD, about 3½ h.

First crossing: as for the first ascensionists of the Rosenhorn.

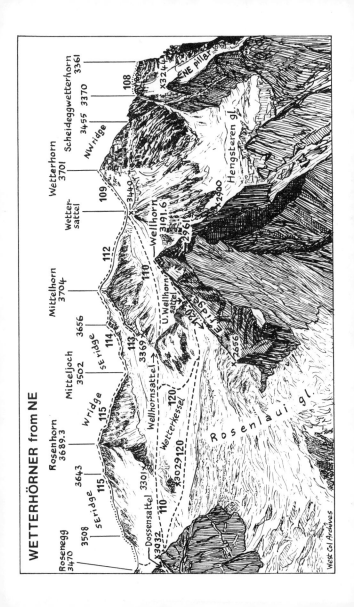

WETTERHÖRNER from NE

Rosenegg 3470
Rosenegg 3508
3643
S ridge
115
Rosenhorn 3689.3
W ridge
115
Mitteljoch 3502
SE ridge
3656
114
Mittelhorn 3704
112
110
113
3369
Wellhorn 3191.6
Wetter-sattel
109
3440
2961
2900
Wetterhorn 3701
NW ridge
3455 3370
Scheideggwetterhorn 3361
108
X3244
NE pillar
Hengsteren gl.

Dossensattel 3301
X3032
110
X3029 120
Wetterkessel
Wellhornsattel
120
U. Wellhorn-sattel
X3190
2656
E spur
Rosenlaui gl.

West Col Archives

Rosenlaui – Gauli – Bächli basins

WELLHORN   3191.6m.

LK 1229, 1230. A massive and towering rock edifice, one of the most imposing summits of secondary height in the Bernese Alps. Together with the Wetterhorn it is one of the two principal objectives offered by the Dossen hut. The rock is limestone and varies from bad to fairly good. The long NE ridge running to the Kl. Wellhorn (2701m.) is the famous Welligrat, first traversed by Gertrude Bell in 1902. This rte. and other technical climbs are described in the "Engelhörner" guide (1968). First ascent: E. von Fellenberg with P. Egger, C. Michel, 31 July, 1866. 2nd ascent: W. A. B. Coolidge with C. & U. Almer, 12 September, 1872.

<u>East Ridge</u>. The usual rte., a well trodden climb, quite sound now, interesting, PD/PD+ owing to the complicated gl. crossing, now much worse than 100 years ago. First ascensionists, but Coolidge party used the traverse across lower snowband.

120 From the Dossen hut follow a track behind the hut to the snowfield under the S ridge of the Dossengrat. Climb steep snow or ice for about 300m. to the Dossensattel at the top, under pt. 3032m. On this section it is usually best to keep R at first, then go more directly in the centre on the last part. Conditions vary considerably, but even in good conditions there is water ice on rock patches. From the saddle descend a couloir for 100m., snow, ice, rock or scree, depending on conditions. Near the bottom bear L on snow and descend to the Rosenlaui gl. Continue bearing L in the direction of the Rosenhorn. Keep in line with a small rock wall surmounted by ice cliffs immediately ahead. This is really an extension of the NE ridge of the Rosenhorn, with a base pt. 3029m. There are now two alternatives.

(1) Continue upwards for a short distance in this direction,

then bear R below séracs towards the Wellhornsattel; there is usually a well-beaten track to mark the way. Before going up the final steep snow slope turn directly down the gl. to the R, keeping well away from rocks on L. Go through an area of large crevasses, then descend a wall of steep broken ice. Continue down this steep, badly crevassed zone to an easier section below; as soon as possible trend up L towards the Unter Wellhornsattel. This is easily recognised as a deep gap in the lower part of the Wellhorn S ridge, just under pt. 2984m. This alternative can be very difficult and complicated, and sometimes owing to ice movement, impossible or too dangerous. However, you cross crevasses at the correct angle, better in this respect than the second alternative ($2\frac{1}{2}$-3 h. from Dossen hut).

(2) Do not continue up the gl. on the normal Wellhornsattel rte. Instead cross the gl. trending somewhat down to the R in line with the Unter Wellhornsattel. In traversing the gl. keep below a line of short ice cliffs which cut across the gl. and seem to merge into an area of rocks. This is the steep section of the first alternative. Continue below this icefall then rise in the line of the saddle. This is not so difficult or as steep as the first approach, but it involves complicated and sometimes difficult crevasse work. The rte. lies parallel with crevasses ($2\frac{1}{2}$-3 h.).

Turn away from the Unter Wellhornsattel and descend near the SE side of the mtn. on snow, keeping the main crevasses to your R. Hug the wall on reaching the pt. where a large obvious snowband lies a short way above. So reach a short snow gully cutting the wall and giving access to the snowband near its upper end. Again, two alternatives.

(1) Continue traversing along base of wall till it is possible to mount a snow/scree terrace. Go R along this and ascend diagonally R over easy slabby rock to the E ridge. Follow the ridge without special difficulty, bits of I+, to the summit.

Reaching the terrace can be difficult and complicated by the state of the crevasses.

(2) Climb the gully indicated above, generally easy, to the snowband. Traverse this R, going slightly downwards, and from near its far end climb slabby rocks to the E ridge and continue to the summit. Devoid of snow, the access gully can be quite unpleasant but it avoids further crevasse complications ($1\frac{1}{2}$-2 h., 4-5 h. from Dossen hut).

DOSSEN   3138.2m.

121 LK 1230. Tossen. This little peak is a popular excursion from the Dossen hut. It has an outlying summit further S, pt. 3144m. Easily reached in 30 min. by a short steep rock ridge from the Dossensattel, Rte. 120. First ascent: F. J. Hugi and party, 13 August, 1828.

RENFENHORN   3259m.

122 LK 1230. Ränfenhorn. Simple summit at a corner of the upper Rosenlaui gl., reached from Rte. 118 in 30 min. above the Renfenjoch ($2\frac{3}{4}$ h. from Dossen hut). First ascent probably R. Noel with A. Jaun, J. Tännler, 29 September, 1868.

HANGENDGLETSCHERHORN   3291.9m.

123 LK 1230. Fine secondary pyramid mtn., half a day from the Gauli hut by the SE flank, Hangend gl. and the short E ridge, F+ (4 h.). First ascent: J. E. Müller, a surveyor, 1788. One of the earliest recorded ascents in the Bernese Alps.

RITZLIHORN   3263.1m.   3282m.

124 LK 1230. A massive rock peak seamed by gullies and ribs, and a magnificent viewpoint. A direct ascent can be made up the SW face above the Mattenalpsee below the Gauli hut, in about 6 h. Grade I/II according to way taken. Rock generally loose everywhere. First climbed by surveyors between 1811-1818. Tourist ascent: H. F. Montgomery, S. Taylor with M. Blatter, K. Steiger, 3 August, 1864.

ANKENBÄLLI 3605m.

125 LK 1229, 1230. An independent summit of snow and rock marking the first pt. on the long ridge running SE from the Berglistock. Not to be confused with its namesake near the Mettenberg in the Schreckhorn group. No special interest. First ascent, 1887.

EWIGSCHNEEHORN 3329.4m.

LK 1230. A magnificent viewpoint, quite popular among parties visiting the Lauteraar hut. The rte. from the Gauli hut ascends the easy but increasingly crevassed Grienbärgli gl. First ascent: E. Desor with J. Leuthold, 1841. Ascended in same year by J. D. Forbes.

<u>South-East Ridge from South</u>. The trade rte., F. It reaches the Gaulipass (c. 3200m.), neither marked nor named on map, and situated NW of pt. 3217m. First ascensionists.

126 From the Lauteraar hut descend by a cut path to the gl. and go along this W then NW for 5 km. to a marker cairn on the R side, indicated by pt. 2561.7m. There is an avalanche cone to R of this ($2\frac{1}{2}$ h.). Keeping L, ascend to near top of cone, then traverse L to rock in an open gully and follow a small track up grass, scree and rocks. Pass the foot of a buttress, pt. 2928m., and continue steeply under the buttress, slanting L to reach the Gaulipass at the top (2 h.). Follow the easy ridge over large blocks and snow to the summit (30 min., 5 h. from Lauteraar hut).

<u>South-East Ridge from North</u>. The ordinary rte. from the Gauli hut, F+.

127 From the Gauli hut follow a small track to the Gauli gl., cross it and climb up the centre of the Grunbergli (Grienbärgli) gl. to the Gaulipass (4 h.), then up the ridge (30 min., $4\frac{1}{2}$ h. from Gauli hut).

GAULIPASS c. 3200m.

LK 1230. Not marked on map, at foot of SE ridge of Ewig-schneehorn. See Rte. 126. One of the oldest regular gl. passes in the Bernese Alps, between the Gauli and Lauteraar basins, first recorded crossing in 1795.

HÜHNERSTOCK NE. 3307m. SW. 3306m.

128 LK 1230. Hienderstock. One of the more bizarre spelling changes by LK, and which summit is highest has been trans-posed again. This double-summit peak rises directly behind the Lauteraar hut and has consequently been climbed by many rtes. In general the rock is an excellent granite, notably smooth, but the original rte. on the NE peak (ESE ridge) has huge delicately poised blocks on it. Once reckoned as the hardest and most dangerous mtn. in the Bernese Alps East area. First ascent: NE peak, W. A. B. Coolidge, F. Gardiner with C. & U. **Almer,** 15 September, 1886. SW peak, A. & H. Baumgartner, A. Körber, Pf. Studer with A. Anderegg, J. Moor, J. Tännler, 10 July, 1889.

Summary, NE peak: ESE ridge from Hiendertelltijoch, III+, pitch of IV+. E rib, IV. N ridge, III. Linking ridge from SW peak, III+ (G. A. Hasler with U. Fuhrer, C. Jossi, 23 September, 1902).

SW peak: SE flank and S ridge, III. W ridge, II+. The Rothoren (3003m.), marking S end of S ridge, directly above hut, has excellent short rtes. up to VI.

BÄCHLISTOCK 3247m.

129 LK 1230. A fine tower-like granite peak, equally accessible from the Lauteraar and Bächli huts. It has a prominent and detached SE summit, 3240m. First ascent: H. Baumgartner, M. Brémond with H. von Bergen, J. Tännler, 27 September, 1888.

Summary: Ordinary Lauteraar hut rte., by E Trift gl. and

SW flank, reaching SE ridge near pt. 3240m., PD (II+). S
ridge of pt. 3240m., III. WNW ridge, III. From Bächli or
Gauli huts, by N ridge, PD (II+).

GROSS DIAMANTSTOCK   3162m.

130 LK 1230. One of the most alluring granite peaks in this
area, commanding a dominant position at the top of the Gauli,
Grueben and Bächli gl. basins; therefore accessible from the
3 huts in these basins. First ascent: C. Montandon and party,
c. 1890. Traversed by G. A. Hasler with U. Fuhrer, C. Jossi,
25 September, 1902.
  Summary: SSW ridge, II+. NW ridge, III+. NE face, IV+.
ENE ridge, III+. SE face and SSW ridge, easiest rte., II-.

KLEIN (CHLYNE) DIAMANTSTOCK   2839. 1m.

131 LK 1230. Attractive rock peak equidistant between the
Bächli and Grueben huts.   Normal rte. by W ridge, easy.
Several good rock climbs.   First ascent as Hasler traverse
party on Gross, above.

ALPLISTOCK   2877.4m.

132 LK 1230.   Rises directly behind (N of) the Bächli hut.
Pleasant rock scrambles. First ascent: F. Gardiner with
P. & R. Almer, 4 July, 1905.

BRANDLAMMHORN   3108m.

133 LK 1230. Fairly important rock peak on S side of Bächli
basin. Rock good on the harder rtes., loose on the easier
ones. First ascent: F. Gardiner with P. & R. Almer, 9 July,
1905.

BRÜNBERG   2982. 1m.

134 LK 1230. After the Gr. Diamantstock, the most important rock peak in the Bächli basin. It has triple summits connected by sharp ridges and a big flying buttress to the N, directly opposite the Bächli hut. These ridges and their facets give excellent rtes. from II to VI. First ascent: L. Liechti, C. Monnard, C. Montandon, 1886.

HÜHNERTÄLIHORN   3179.4m.

135 LK 1230. Hiendertelltihorn. Another monstrous spelling, cf. Rte. 128. A regular granite pyramid standing on the ridge between the Gauli and Grueben basins. Easiest rtes., II+. First ascent: H. Kümmerly, C. Montandon, 24 September, 1888.

Unteraar – Oberaar – Galmi basins

STUDERHORN   3638m.

LK 1249, 1250. A splendid little snow peak, one of the most interesting in any of the Aar gl. basins. Very popular and short snow/ice climbs, increasingly complicated by crevasses. Magnificent close-up view of the Finsteraarhorn. First ascent: R. Lindt, G. Studer with J. & K. Blatter, P. Sulzer, 5 August, 1864. The mtn. was named by Agassiz in honour of Bernard Studer, a cousin of Gottlieb, and a companion of J. D. Forbes. So it is fitting that the other and perhaps greater Studer should climb it. Winter ascents, etc. Details fail. Rpt. Talbot, 1968, 1969.

<u>Traverse by South-East Flank and North-West Ridge</u>. A first class outing, entirely on snow. PD. SE flank by first ascensionists.

136 From the Oberaarjoch hut go up the Studerfirn, below the U. Studerjoch, to the foot of the steep SE flank. Climb diagonally R above a rockband coming out from the U. Studerjoch, then trend L up a steep snow slope near rock further L to reach the broad crest at the top of the slope. Follow the broad ridge with a few rocks to summit ($2\frac{3}{4}$ h.). Go straight down the narrow and sometimes corniced NW ridge to the O. Studerjoch (3416m.) (30 min.), and return by the Studerfirn ($1\frac{1}{2}$ h., $4\frac{3}{4}$ h. for round trip).

<u>North-East Ridge</u>. A mixed climb, PD+. The rock is very loose. First ascent: A. W. Moore, H. Walker with J. & M. Anderegg, 29 June, 1872.

137 From the Aar biv. hut cross the gl. junction due S towards the foot of the ridge (2668m.) (45 min.). Bear SE into the steep gl. bay on the L, keeping L to avoid its lower crevasses.

Move into the centre of the crevassed bay, then traverse R and climb a vague rib which is just L of a snow tongue rising towards the crest of the NE ridge on this side. The snow tongue reaches the ridge above pt. 3066m. So reach the crest of the ridge ($1\frac{1}{2}$ h.). Climb the rock crest, steep but not really difficult, then snow at the edge of the N face, up to a fine snow ridge which leads with interest, cornices on R, to an easing in the angle. Join the ordinary rte. near the summit (2 h., about $4\frac{1}{4}$ h. from Aar biv. hut).

Note: In 1966 J. O. Talbot found it impossible to traverse R on to the vague rib and reach the crest, because of gl. shrinkage, leaving a wall of very smooth rock. There was also a huge schrund at this pt.

<u>North Face</u>. A superb ice climb, one of the best in the Bernese Alps, with almost no objective danger. Average angle, 49°, with pitches of 60° or more possible. D+/TD-, 600m. The rock rib almost in the summit line and twisting R at bottom, which is L of the original rte., is of the same standard, the rock being poor and giving pitches of IV (E. Saxer, H. P. Trachsel, 23 September, 1971). After an intermediate area of rock L of the main central rib, another rib is formed L again, which curves up to join the upper part of the NE ridge. The ice channel between this rib and the intermediate rock area gives a climb of D/D+ at 50° to near the top of the NE ridge (H. & M. Bächli, 22 July, 1971).

First ascent: P. Bonnant, Mlle. L. Boulaz, 1 August, 1940. 2nd ascent and descent of face: M. Brandt, A. & R. Voillat, 16-17 September, 1956. First British (7th) ascent: J. O. Talbot with M. Epp, 28 August, 1966. In winter: H. Lüssi, W. Manz, W. Stoll, 2-3 January, 1970. Climbed over 30 times by one rte. or another at end of 1977.

138 From the Aar biv. cross the gl. junction S to the foot of the NE ridge, pt. 2668m., then work up the L side of the icefall below the rocky areas of the N face, falling ice possible and some crevasse problems, to the centre foot of the face beyond the summit line rib. The bergschrund is usually bridged early in the season and may be multiple. Later on it can be very difficult to cross (1 h.).

Above the bergschrund climb the steep ice slope trending L, up grooved and ribbed ice runnels. The best line varies according to conditions. By keeping L, a low ice wall is avoided. At mid-height there is a distinct ice rib and you keep L of this. Further up, climb direct then turn a bulge in the face below the summit by moving R, and L of a rock outcrop just below the NW ridge. At least two parties have finished direct, but here there is usually an ice wall and a cornice (6-8 h. from foot of face, has been climbed in $3\frac{1}{2}$ h.).

ALTMANN 3468m.

LK 1250. Secondary summit on the main ridge between the Studerhorn and Oberaarhorn. Rarely climbed. J. G. Altmann was a mid-18th century glaciologist. See Oberaarhorn below.

OBERAARHORN 3637m.

LK 1250. Topographically an important mtn. but ranking below the first order in mountaineering interest. Virtually climbed by one rte., the other ridges and faces having been done only a few times. First ascent: L. Stephen with M. Anderegg, 23 August, 1860. On ski: Reichert, Schottelius, 28 May, 1901. The W ridge (AD) from the summit to the Altmann was traversed by W. Baumgartner, H. Schneider, 2 August, 1911. The NE ridge, and all the ridge from the Scheuchzerhorn over the Grunerhorn (q. v.) to the summit (AD+) was traversed by W. Baumgartner, H. Schneider, 1 August, 1911. The more tempting SW face (PD+) was climbed direct by M. Brandt, A. Voillat, 22 July, 1958 (3 h.).

South Ridge. A trade rte., climbed by all-comers. F. First ascensionists.

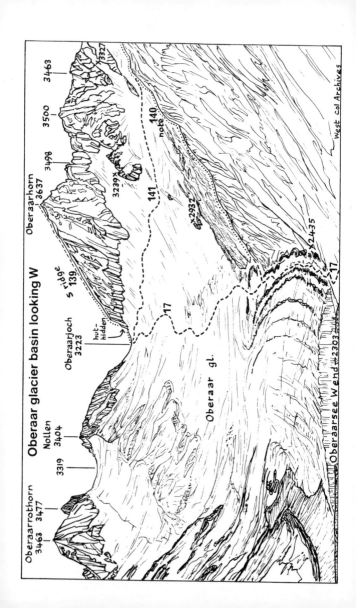

139 From the Oberaarjoch hut climb steep scree and rocks with traces of a path to a broad snow ridge, quite steep, which leads to the top (1¼ h. from hut).

OBERAARJOCH   3223m.

LK 1250. Fine gl. pass between the Oberaarhorn and Nollen (3404m.). See Rte. 17. First recorded traverse by J. H. Weiss & party, 1797. On ski: V. de Beauclair, Ehlert, W. Loh-müller, Mönnichs, W. Paulcke, 19 January, 1897 - an historic early ski crossing.

GRUNERHORN   3436m.

LK 1250. A snowcap on the long ridge between the Oberaarhorn and Scheuchzerhorn. The first party traversing this ridge (see Oberaarhorn above) pointed out that the nameless rock pt. 3500m. situated much closer to the Oberaarhorn is the more prominent summit and the name Grunerhorn should be transferred to it. However this suggestion has been ignored. Little mountaineering interest except for a good technical rte. on the NW face by G. C. van der Leek, D. L. Wansink, 8 July, 1958, about D/D+. G. S. Gruner was a mid-18th century glaciologist. First ascent as Scheuchzerhorn below.

SCHEUCHZERHORN   3462m.

LK 1250. A fairly frequented snow peak, mostly from the Lauteraar hut. Accessible from the Oberaar hut by a long gl. traverse over badly crevassed slopes. The NW face is a very good snow/ice and mixed climb, recommended, D/D+. M. Brandt, R. Theytaz, R. Voillat, 13 September, 1960. J. J. Scheuchzer was an early 18th century glaciologist. First ascent: E. J. Häberlin with A. & J. von Weissenfluh, 30 July, 1872.

<u>North-West Ridge (from Scheuchzerjoch)</u>. The usual rte. from the Lauteraar hut, a very good snow climb with crevasse and cornice problems. PD/PD+. First ascensionists.

140 From the Lauteraar hut cross the moraine and ice of the Unteraar gl., sometimes with swift-flowing surface streams, to the narrow cwm entrance below the Scheuchzerjoch. Climb the rough unpleasant cwm bed, better with old snow, to below a barrier supporting the gl. and stretching right across the cwm. Normally turn this on the extreme L, but in certain snowy conditions it has been found easier on the R side. Continue trending R up to a little gl. plateau at 2600m. Now go up the main Tierberg gl. trending L, crevassed and often icy, and halfway up bear a little R to a bergschrund near the top which is crossed to reach the final slope and the Scheuchzerjoch (3072m.) (2½ h.). Ascend easy crevassed slopes W, passing below (S of) the rock spur of pt. 3352m., and gradually bear R to join the NW ridge by a short steep snow slope behind pt. 3352m. Follow the narrow and often corniced snow crest to the summit (1½ h., 4 h. from Lauteraar hut).

Coming from the Berghaus Oberaar, the Scheuchzerjoch can be reached by going up the obvious large moraine, then a gl. tongue, both coming down SE to the Oberaar gl. (6½ h. from inn to summit).

<u>South-East Ridge.</u> The shortest rte. from the Oberaarjoch hut. F+.

141 Traverse the badly crevassed but otherwise easy upper slopes of the Oberaar gl., below the Oberaarhorn and Grunerhorn, at c.3050m., to the foot of the ridge (1¾ h.). Go up snow below R side of ridge for 50m., then climb a broken rock depression to the broad crest which is reached just above pt. 3228m. Continue up easy rocks then snow directly to the summit (1¼ h., 3 h. from hut).

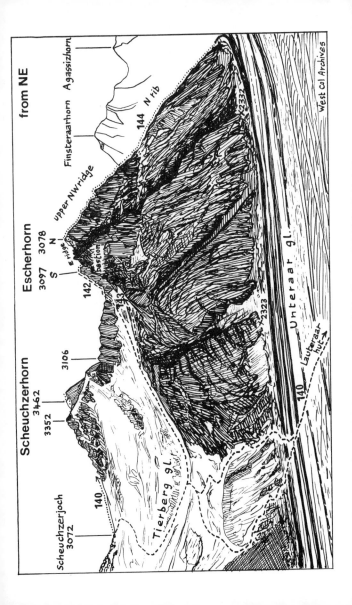

ESCHERHORN   N. 3078m.   S. 3097m.

LK 1250. Conspicuous, angular rock peak of complex struct-
ure, overlooking the junction of the Lauteraar, Finsteraar and
Unteraar gls., and detached N of the main ridge near the
Scheuchzerhorn. Mainly composed of sound red granite, quite
smooth, its climbs compare for quality with the Hühnerstock
(Hienderstock). Climbed frequently from the Lauteraar hut.
A. Escher was an early 19th century Swiss scientist. First
ascent: G.W. Young with J. Lochmatter; H. Young with C.
Ruppen, 6 August, 1904.

<u>South Ridge.</u> The ordinary rte. to the S peak, PD. The con-
tinuation ridge to N peak, the summit proper, is AD (III+).

142 From the Lauteraar hut follow Rte. 140 to the first plateau
of the Tierberg gl. at c. 2600m. Traverse the gl. WNW, crevasses in same direction, and reach a ridge gap just S of
pt. 3097m. by a short steep broken gully slanting R. Now
follow the steep pleasant ridge with short bits of II to pt. 3097m.
(4 h.).

To continue, descend a sharp rock crest with pitches of III/
III+ to a small gap. Climb a pitch out of the gap and continue
along the fine and exposed crest, down to gap 3043.7m. Now
ascend the final part of the crest with two pitches of III+ to
pt. 3078m. (1½ h., 5½ h. from Lauteraar hut).

<u>East Ridge.</u> This ridge terminates abruptly at a high level in
a steep bastion. Above this the main crest has small pinnacles
and is relatively easy. Reaching this crest constitutes the
main difficulty. The quickest descent from the mtn. is by
abseiling down the indirect rte. as described below. First
ascensionists used the indirect rte.

143 From the Lauteraar hut approach as for Rtes. 140, 142,
but once the rising traverse has been started on the Tierberg
gl., soon move further R on to a bordering snow/screefield
giving access to a large sloping terrace under the S side of the
E ridge. Cross this ground easily to below ridge. About 40m.

L of the bastion terminating the ridge above, reach the first of several chimney/gullies cutting the S wall of the ridge. Direct rte. Climb this first chimney/gully (III+) to a shoulder on the R. Straight above, take a short stiff pitch (IV+) then move L across a steep wall to a crack slanting R up to ridge crest (IV+, sustained). Now follow crest over large blocks and little pinnacles (II) to summit. Indirect rte. From the first chimney/gully work L below S wall of ridge to the last chimney/gully somewhat R of the summit line. Either climb this direct to ridge above, or climb steep rock L of it for 2/3 rds. of the height, then enter and finish up gully (IV-, mainly III). A few min. on ridge remain to summit (4½ h. from Lauteraar hut).

144 North-West Flank and North-West Ridge. Follows the large sweep of slabs past pt. 2493.7m. in a direct line to the upper NW ridge, pt. 2863m. Fine variable slab climbing. The upper ridge crest has three short tower/steps, all excellent climbing, none of which can be done below III+. The N rib, bordering W side of the huge N gully can be climbed on fine slabs (IV/IV+) to the upper NW ridge at pt. 2863m. (About 2½-4 h. from gl. to summit).

HINTERER TIERBERG   3205m.

VORDER TIERBERG   3111m.

145 LK 1250. Part of the long granite ridge running E from the Scheuchzerhorn into the terminal double Zinggenstock summits (3041m.). Interesting rock climbs and scrambles on fair to good granite, directly accessible across the Unteraar gl. from the Lauteraar hut.

NOLLEN   3404m.

LK 1250. Not named on map, large hump forming a step in ridge between the Oberaarrothorn and Oberaarjoch. No interest.

OBERAARROTHORN   W. 3477m.   E. 3463m.

LK 1250. Rock peak between the Oberaarjoch and Galmilücke.
No interest.

VORDERES GALMIHORN   3517m.

HINTERES GALMIHORN   3486m.

LK 1250. Attractive twin snow/rock peaks, popular from the
Oberaarjoch hut.   Both can be climbed separately but it is
hardly more effort to traverse them. They are separated by
the Bächilücke (3386m.). First ascent: A. Barbey, L. Kurz
with two guides, 12 July, 1884.

Traverse: A pleasant climb with a rock ridge on the lower
peak. PD. First ascensionists.

146 From the Oberaarjoch hut descend round the W foot of the
Nollen and Oberaarrothorn over generally crevassed slopes
and continue straight up the easy NW slopes of the Vord. Galmihorn, twisting through crevasse zones and low ice walls to
reach the summit direct, cornice on other side ($2\frac{3}{4}$ h.). Now
descend N over a broad snow shoulder, cornices on R, to the
Bächilücke saddle (30 min.). Continue on scree, snow then a
rock crest with little snowy saddles to the Hint. Galmihorn
(45 min.).   Descend the N ridge, over pt. 3466m., latterly a
nice rock crest with bits of II to the snowy Galmilücke (3293m.)
(30 min.). From here descend easily on snow to the approach
rte. under W ridge of Oberaarrothorn, hence the hut (45 min.,
$5\frac{1}{4}$ h. for round trip).

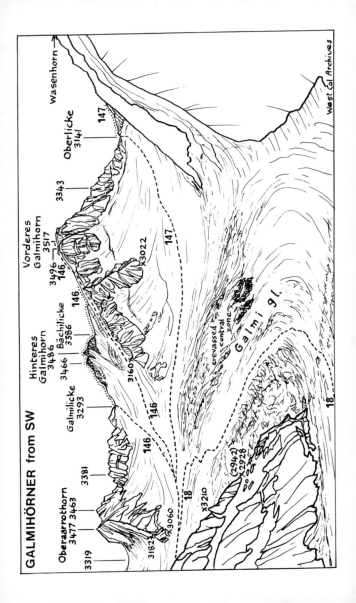

GALMIHÖRNER from SW

Wasenhorn →

Oberlicke
3141

147

3343

Vorderes
Galmihorn
3517

147

x3022

3496
146

146

Hinteres
Galmihorn
3486

Bächlicke
3386

146

Galmilicke
3293

3466

31607

146

146

146

Oberaarrothorn
3477 3463

3381

3060

18

3319

31827

x3210

(2942)
x2928

18

Galmi gl.

crevassed
central
zone

18

West Col Archives

WASENHORN   3446.8m.

LK 1250.   A secondary peak but a good vantage pt. for the
Fiescher gl. basin.   It has rock and ice climbs of some im-
portance, notably the NW face, 550m. , D; M. Brandt, A. &
R. Voillat, 21 July, 1958. First ascent: Hr. & Fr. Tauscher-
Geduly with A. Pinggera, J. Reinstadler, 14 August, 1885.

North-East Ridge. A pleasant mixed climb, F+. First ascensionists.

147 From the Oberaarjoch hut approach as for Rte. 146. Take
a lower line down the Galmi gl. and give the NW spur of the
Vord. Galmihorn a wide berth.   Return S below this spur and
climb the large crevassed gl. hollow above to a bergschrund
and the Oberlücke (3141m.) (2 h.). Now follow the rock ridge
over pt. 3302m. to a snow section leading to more rocks and
a forepeak. Continue over a twist in the crest to summit (1½ h. ,
3½ h. from hut).

Addenda

BERNESE ALPS CENTRAL

Following publication of the 1/25,000 map sheet 1268 Lötschental in May, 1978, the following mostly minor differences can be noted compared with the guidebook text.

R = route number (not page number).

R8, 9   Heimritz in the Gasteretal (sic) reads 1635m.

R18   Hochenalp reads 2048m.

R19   Lauchernalp reads 2106m.

R20   Weritzstafel (sic)

R21   Tellistafel (sic)

R22   Gletscherstafel roadhead reads 1763m. Gletscherstafel bridge, 1771m.

R33   Stockhorn hut reads 2598m.

R76   Lötschenpass. The lowest pt. of this pass is measured as 2678m., some distance SW of the hut at 2690m. where the regular path crosses.

R77   Hockenhorn reads 3293.0m. Kleinhockenhorn (sic), 3163m.

R145, 152 Pt. at foot of upper ridge reads 3706m.

R146   Foot of ridge reads 3173m.

R147   Base pt. of broad rib reads 3040m.

R155   Baltschiederjoch reads 3204m.

R161   Ridge access marker pt. reads 3624m. However, lowest access pt. to ridge now indicated as 3551m.

R167   Baltschiederlücke reads 3219m.

R177   Distlig gl. reads Dischlig gl.

Numerous other phonetic spellings. The following may also be reported.

R2   Doldenhorn hut. Reconstruction in 1979 will reduce number of sleeping places from 48 to 44, but the dining room capacity, at present 30, will be increased to seating for 47.

R29   Jungfraujoch. The scheme to build a new hotel complex with a rotating restaurant having a seating capacity of 600 (? !) received cantonal approval in 1978. Mountaineering bodies opposed to the scheme are appealing to central government. If the plan goes ahead, accommodation and regulations applying to climbers staying at the Jungfraujoch will change - possibly for the worse.

R47   Doldenhorn SE face direct. It is worth noting that the late Nick Estcourt was only 15 years old when he made this grade IV+ ascent with the guide Hans Hari.

R124   It appears that all published references since 1932 attributing the presence of H. Rudy in the first ascent party are incorrect. He was not present, as shown by the research in "Welzenbach's Climbs". This error has been perpetuated as a result of a misunderstood conversation between Hans Lauper and Welzenbach, which was widely reported in the climbing press during 1933 - E. B. R. corresp. June, 1978.

R170   Preamble. Schulz = Schulze.

             British ascent, for 12 July read 21 July.

R179   Schinhorn. The grade is PD.

BERNESE ALPS EAST

R11   Strahlegg hut. The new building is to be called Schreckhorn hut, and will be erected below the old at 2520m. The number of sleeping places will be increased to 94 and the dining room capacity is to be doubled.

R41   First winter solo ascent by T. Hasegawa, 3-9 March, 1978. 48 h. later solo by Ivan Ghirardini, in 6 days. Several winter ascents were made in March, 1978.

R77, 78   The reporting nearly 20 years ago of the Smith-Wakefield ascent of the Fiescherwand has to date been incorrectly assigned to the Welzenbach rte. Correspondence, photostats of original documents, and an unpublished account of the Scottish ascent of the NE rib are now in the West Col Archives, courtesy of Brian Wakefield.

R. G. C.   ·September, 1978

INDEX OF ROUTES SHOWN ON DIAGRAMS

Route No.	Diagram on page(s)	Route No.	Diagram on page(s)
2	49	42	56
3	35	43	56
4	49	44	56, 59
5	54	45	56, 59
6	38, 46	46	46, 69, 74
7	92	47	69, 72
9	92, 100	48	69, 72, 100
10	100	49	69, 72
11	111	50	69, 72
12	135	51	72, 87
17	156	53	74
18	163	54	74
19	100	55	72, 87
25	38, 46	56	72, 82
26	38	57	82, 87
27	38	58	87
28	38, 43, 49	59	69, 72, 92
29	38, 49	60	69, 72, 92
30	43, 49	61	69, 72, 92
31	43, 49	62	92
32	43	64	72
33	49	65	72
34	46, 69	69	94, 100
35	46	71	82
36	49	72	82
37	38, 49, 54	73	104
38	54	74	100
39	54, 59	75	82
40	59	76	100
41	56	77	82, 100, 104

Route No.	Diagram on page(s)	Route No.	Diagram on page(s)
78	100, 104	105	111
79	100, 102, 104	108	135, 139, 145
80	100, 102, 104	109	135, 139, 145
81	102, 104	110	145
82	102, 104	111	135, 139
83	100	112	135, 139, 145
85	111, 120	113	145
86	120, 135, 139	114	135, 139, 145
87	111, 120	115	135, 139, 145
88	120	116	139
89	111, 120	117	139
90	120, 139	118	139
92	111, 115, 120, 132	120	145
93	111, 115, 132	136	102, 104
94	111	137	104
95	111, 120	138	104
96	120	139	156
97	120	140	156, 159
99	115	141	156
100	111, 120, 132	142	159
101	111, 132	143	159
102	111, 115, 120, 132	144	159
103	111	146	163
104	132	147	163

General Index

Aar biv. hut   30
Agassizhorn   97
Agassizjoch   97
Alplistock   151
Altmann   155
Ankenbälli   100,149

Bächilücke   162
Bächlistock   150
Bächlital hut   34
Bergli hut   25
Berglijoch   143
Berglistock   142
Brandlammhorn   151
Brünberg   151

Diamantstock, Gr.   151
- Kl.   151
Dossen   148
Dossen hut   33

Eiger   50
- Kl.   48
Eiger Gl. Sta.   23
Eigerjoch, Nördl.   48
- Südl.   39,48
Eigerwand   60
Escherhorn   160
Ewigschneehorn   149

Faulberg   93
Fiescher Gabelhorn   93

Fiescherhorn, Gr. 68
- Hint. 68
- Kl. see Ochs
Fiescherjoch 83,95
Fiechersattel 70,71
Fiescherwand 75
Finsteraarhorn 98
- hut 26
Finsteraarjoch 96
Finsteraarrothorn 109
Flesch shelter 27

Gabelhornsattel 93
Galmihorn, Hint. 162
- hut 33
- Vord. 162
Galmilücke 162
Gauli hut 34
Gaulipass 149,150
Gemslücke 32
Gleckstein hut 29
Grueben hut 34
Grünegghorn 88,89
Grunerhorn 157
Grünhorn, Gr. 88
- Kl. 88,89,91
Grünhornlücke 27,91
- Kl. 71
Guggi hut 23
Gwächten 112
Gwächtjoch 113

Hangendgletscherhorn 148
Hiendertelltijoch 150
Hugihorn 131

Hühnerstock 150
Hühnertalihorn 152
Husegg hut 31

Jungfraujoch 23, 36

Kamm 93
Konkordia hut 26

Lauteraarhorn 126
- Kl. 131
Lauteraar hut 30
Lauteraar-Rothörner 131
Lauteraarsattel 114

Mettenberg 110
Mittelhorn 140
Mitteljoch 141
Mittellegi hut 24
Mönch 36
Mönchjoch, O. 25, 45
- U. 25, 48

Nässihorn 114
Nässijoch 119, 122
- U. 112
Nollen 161

Oberaarhorn 155
Oberaarjoch, hut 31, 32, 157
Oberaarrothorn 162
Oberaarsee inn 31
Oberlücke 164
Ochs 71, 80

Renfenhorn 144, 148
Ritzlihorn 148
Rosenegg 141, 142
Rosenhorn 141

Rosenlaui biv. hut   33
Rothoren   150

Scheidegg, Kl.   23
Scheideggwetterhorn   133
Scheuchzerhorn   157
Scheuchzerjoch   158
Schönbühlhorn   93
Schreckhorn   116
- Kl.   112
Stieregg inn   88
Strahlegghorn   130
Strahlegg hut   28
Strahleggpass   130
Studerhorn   153
Studerjoch, Ob.   108

Tierberg, Hint.   161
- Vord.   161
Trugberg   45

Walcherhorn   68
Wannenhorn, Gr.   93
- Kl.   95
Wasenhorn   164
Wellhorn   146
- Kl.   146
Wetterhorn   136
Wetterlimmi   144
Wettersattel   137,138

Zinggenstock   161